Make Haste Slowly

Second Edition

Donald K. Smith

Growing meaningful communication within and between differing cultures

BOOKS ON

CREATING UNDERSTANDING

Copies may be ordered through
booksoncreatingunderstanding.com

MAKE HASTE SLOWLY

© 1984, First Edition (Nine printings)

© 2011, Second Edition (First printing)

by Donald K. Smith

Italics in Scripture quotations are the author's emphasis.

Unless otherwise indicated, Scripture quotations are from
The Holy Bible, New International Version (NIV)
©1973, 1984 by International Bible Society,
used by permission of Zondervan Publishing House

Other Scripture quotations are from:
Holy Bible, New Living Translation (NLT)
©1996, 2004 by Tyndale Charitable Trust.
Used by permission of Tyndale House Publishers.
All rights reserved.

The author expresses appreciation to Condeo Press (www.condeopress.com) for introducing him to Snowfall Press serving as the printing house for his books.

Dr. and Mrs. Smith are now serving in Africa at Daystar University
More information about Daystar is available at
Daystar University: http://www.daystar.ac.ke
DaystarUS: http://www.daystarus.org

§

Contents

Part Five: Stimulating Change

Part Six: Does Change Mean Progress?

§

Preface

(First Edition)

Every book is the result of many different streams of thought, experience, and challenge. The perceptions and tactics introduced in *Make Haste Slowly* also result from the fusion of many different ideas, disappointments, and small successes, covering a period of thirty years living and working on the African continent.

Fresh inputs in struggling with old problems came through insightful professors at the University of Oregon. Matabele friends in Zimbabwe helped to refine the ore gained in graduate study so that we together could benefit. From there, others began to ask to share in the results—to help their service come closer to their own desires. As seminars and consultations spread, a plan for teaching developed that became Daystar Communications. Intensive institutes drew leaders from more than thirty-five countries of Africa, Asia, Latin America, and Europe. They too, helped to refine and shape these concepts. Those programs continued to develop and are now Daystar University College in Nairobi, Kenya.

But most of the material was not available apart from the special training sessions until the Lutheran World Federation requested our participation in a major research study, the Communication for Development Project centered in southern Sudan. Parallel to the CDP research, the major development agency there, Norwegian Church Aid, requested substantial help in extensive aid projects. The resulting series of workshops for Norwegian and Sudanese staff led to a request for the material in a written form.

So it was that *Make Haste Slowly* was written as a response to the challenge of a specific setting. Many of the illustrations are consequently from that context. But the principles are equally applicable in urban settings, in rural areas, and for development work—or for fuller obedience to Christ's command to go and tell the Good News to all men.

Portland, Oregon, USA

1984

§

Preface

(Second Edition)

After nine printings and use of *Make Haste Slowly* far
beyond the anticipated audience, it's time to reflect the wider
audience, improving the flow of thought and breadth of
illustrations. Teaching (and learning from it) in North
America, Asia, and Europe has clarified and reinforced the
importance of these simple principles. The beginning
programs have now grown into Daystar University with
campuses in Nairobi, Athi River, and Mombasa, Kenya.

I'm grateful to Lutheran World Federation and Norwegian
Church Aid in Sudan for the challenges of the
Communication for Development Project that led to this
book. Among the many individuals to whom I am indebted
are Karl Johan Lundstrom for many hours of discussion and
application of these principles in South Sudan within the
fine fieldwork done by Dr. David Kitonga, Dr. Jane Odhuno
Awiti, and Rhoda Achieng Ondeng, Katie Baldwin for her
spirit of helps and creative energy in developing this edition,
Dr. Dan Sharp and Thomas Womack for final editing.
Though I wrote the book, it was developed jointly over many
years with my wife Faye as we studied and talked through
many perplexing situations living in the differing cultures of
South Africa, Zimbabwe, and Kenya.

Revisions and additions have been made to better give assistance to the many who've found the principles useful in urban and rural areas of Africa, Asia, Europe, and North and South America. The simple principles have provided a foundation for productive relationships, effective in short and long term efforts to introduce God's *shalom*. In the relationships developed, true sharing of the living Jesus can become vibrantly real, opening the way to the peace and wholeness God intends for man.

Donald K. Smith
Portland, Oregon. USA.
November, 2011

§

**It may not be too much to claim
that the future of our world will depend
on how we deal with identity and difference.**

<small>MIROSLAV VOLF, Bosnian-born theologian</small>

§

Consider the power of wealth and technology, the power of knowledge, power to travel and enter virtually any society, any part of the world. What is the effect of that power on others? Can you help without destroying?

You bring better mastery of the environment, better health, better food, better education, a better future for the children. How important is it that your powerful culture replaces and even disintegrates other ways of life? How can you share your good things without robbing others of their treasures? Or must this be the price of progress?

In the northwest corner of the United States, a majestic site was destroyed in 1957. It was "progress." An ancient fishing and trading center was submerged by a great dam, extending a waterway into the interior and generating power for cities and industries, but destroying a way of life. It's a striking case of cultures in conflict. Are there ways to diminish such unintended consequences?

Chapter One

Listen... Listen... Listen!

At Celilo Falls the massive Columbia River turns on edge, forcing the mile-wide river to rush between basalt cliffs only 140 feet apart. Century after century, great Chinook salmon runs have hesitated here before leaping the falls and continuing their incredible journey to inland tributaries to spawn another generation. For 15,000 years the salmon were netted from dangerous platforms stretching out over the edge of the falls. The catch sustained tribes like the Wasco, Wishram, Cayuse, Nez Perce, Pauite, and Salish, and was traded for goods from dozens of other tribes from Alaska to Arizona. Indian peoples traveling across hundreds of miles of valleys, deserts, and mountains gathered here to trade for obsidian (to make arrowheads and knives), cedar bark cloth, intricately created baskets, deer and elk hides, turquoise, and dried salmon. Celilo was one of the great marketplaces of North America. Lewis and Clark were amazed at the dense and prosperous population in "a great emporium where all the neighboring nations assemble."

Then new ways came with a new race from the East. They built different marketplaces, traded for different goods. Celilo was an interesting and exciting curiosity, but it didn't contribute to new towns, schools, churches. It was dispensable. The men, women, and children depending on Celilo for their very lives somehow were not even seen, except in photographs.

The river must be tamed—so great barges could carry the fruit of the land unhindered to the cities of the West and to ports across the world. The energy of the Columbia must power industries and light the homes and factories of the new Western cities. Another Celilo village would be built, they promised, with new schools and homes.

Now Celilo Falls are gone, silenced and buried by dammed-up waters. The marketplace for a quarter of a continent has dwindled to a few houses below a freeway. Poverty is there, and hopelessness. Even the memories are dim and becoming dimmer. Silence settles on the river instead of the roar of Celilo and the babble of dozens of languages recounting their long journeys to exchange goods from the Great Basin, the western valleys, the mountains, and even the frozen northlands.

Now a few children play in dusty spaces. Adequate schools still have not been built. There are almost no jobs for the men who remain, and few salmon are caught for the women to dry. The rich languages of the past are not heard. A whole way of life was destroyed, and the people broken and cast aside.

Why did this happen? It really is quite simple. A dominant culture overpowered the resident culture, and the dominating ones determined what would happen and when. The Celilo way of life, their ideas and dreams, were considered of little value. Power to resist was absent, so the more powerful forced their way on another people. The newcomers could see little of permanent value in the Celilo culture, little that was worth preserving in the face of their grand schemes for progress. What was this old marketplace worth compared to great stores, shipyards, and nuclear energy? A few dried salmon didn't compare to the value of their irrigated crops. The old trails were nothing compared to their great highways. The things being developed were more significant than the people being destroyed.

Consider: Were the newcomers heartless? Had they no concern for the people who were there first? Did they not know compassion?

They were not heartless; they had compassion for what they understood, and they had concern for the individuals they came to know. There were Christians among them, and they cared much about the Indians' well-being, at least their eternal well-being. Nevertheless, *they didn't understand the way of life being destroyed.* They were in a hurry to build a prosperous way of life, and to bring these others into their pattern of life and belief. Even the missionaries seemed uncaring. They did not listen. They did not learn. They did not *make haste slowly.*

May our sensitivity and understanding of those whom we would help increase — and keep us from more "Celilos" around the world.

PART ONE

Why Bring Change?

What is your motivation for attempting to change another society? What ways do you follow to achieve your goals for others?

There are many motivations, most of them commendable. Perhaps you're moved by compassion, after learning of oppressive poverty, disease, and deprivation enslaving millions or billions worldwide. Or you may be conscious of the privileged material life your culture has developed, so you feel compelled to show others how to have these good things. It may well be that the spiritual blindness of billions who follow false gods compels you to instruct them in God-given Truth. You're not among those who look for new ways to plunder the resources of other peoples, increasing your own power.

You want to help.

How best to do that is the challenge.

Chapter Two

Mapping the Journey

Introducing fundamental change into another group or society is complex. It's easiest to do only a small part of what needs to be done, while pretending that's all that really matters. So a little part of the need is met by a certain group of specialists, a different part by another band of enthusiasts, and new programs are introduced; but other parts of the need are left untouched. Even when the Christian message is the central concern, that message is too often left undemonstrated and thus unheard.

Wholeness in mission is essential. The spiritual must be confirmed by meeting health needs, by encouraging the dignity of self-respect. Fighting famine must not squeeze out the feeding of hearts and minds. All of it must be done together, each part inseparable from all others.

Wholeness in mission is more than each specialist adding his concerns to the total list of activities, then pasting it together under one administrator. It's very different from aid and advice lavishly dispensed by a skilled and powerful organization of professional development people. Wholeness in mission happens only when the people being helped are participants in the change process. It doesn't matter if the change desired is spiritual, social, or physical. Without trust and full participation between "helped" and "helper," the best efforts will result only in superficial change. It's unlikely to be permanent or spread very far in the society. It may, in fact, simply be rejected.

People are not a blackboard on which we draw our designs, but participants in change. They must be involved in determining priorities, choosing personnel, and carrying out programs jointly planned and accepted. How we develop communication that makes possible wholeness in mission is the purpose of this small book.

This book is for the many who are putting their lives into the effort to communicate with very different people. It's useful to the medical worker, the agriculturalist, the teacher, and the Christian evangelist. Whether their involvement in another culture is short-term or for a lifetime, following these basic principles will smooth friction at the meeting point of cultures.

No marvelous formulas are given. No quick and easy path to follow is mapped out. But fruitful ways to begin building effective communication across cultural differences are suggested. When these suggestions are followed, don't expect immediate change; even going about it in the best way is difficult and slow—for both sides! Perhaps one of the most alluring myths is to think that with right knowledge, everything will happen quickly. Attempting too much too quickly can, in fact, slow down and even destroy the foundations for giving and receiving assistance to others.

Two different approaches are possible when seeking to introduce change in such situations: 1) "Attack" a society, virtually forcing it to leave its traditions and social structures so it can become "modernized" and "Christian." 2) Learn how the society is structured, how it operates to make its own decisions, then penetrate the society and stimulate change from within.

The first way has often been used, as at Celilo Falls. Outside change agents have shown little reluctance to force a society to change. Well-intentioned government workers, for example, have recommended special taxes that would make it necessary for peasant farmers to plant cash crops; police and soldiers were then utilized to make sure the taxes were paid, the crops grown, and government orders followed. Even the occasional missionary has complained, "We can never win these people until their culture is broken." Traditional culture patterns have been seen as obstacles that must be flattened before desired change can happen.

There are many examples of the apparent success of this approach in modernizing peoples and in developing cash economies and booming cities in Africa and Asia. A new generation of leaders has emerged who seem to regard traditional culture values less highly than their elders. They're trying to lead their people "into the modern world." The good work of these leaders is valuable.

However, some successes have blinded us to those who have lost their roots and are perplexed by new demands. Old culture patterns have been broken, and along with them, the guidelines for life. The cost of broken communication networks is most clearly seen in the human wreckage around growing cities of the Third World. It can also be seen in rural areas crowded with women, children, and old people; the men have gone to the cities to find new ways to satisfy new desires. Instead, vast slums have been formed by these who have been cast aside by rapidly changing societies. They become reservoirs of recruits for political violence, bringing crime and insecurity to everyone.

There is a better way! Genuine development will come when ideas for change are planted within the society, utilizing its existing communication networks. Change comes from within as people discuss the possibilities and jointly decide what they can do and how they can do it best. The outsider is needed to give new ideas and show new possibilities, but only insiders can create significant movement for any kind of development—social, economic, or spiritual.

Development demands full understanding by the people. Understanding will come through discussions, questions, and group decision to try new ways. The only way this kind of participation can be gained is for the innovator—the outsider—to first listen and learn, entering into the life and heart of the people, earning the right to introduce new ideas.

If you're in a hurry to bring change…learn to go slowly.

Massive changes are shattering traditional societies. Those who lived on land occupied by untold family generations before them are now part of the ferment in the sprawling cities of Asia, Africa, and Latin America. What do they bring with them? What have they left behind? How are they changing in order to survive in totally new environments? Traditional approaches to a society are now seldom useful, but what *will* be effective?

Go slowly, and carefully learn the new situations, the new opportunities—so you can build with solid understanding, and build *with* the people.

Basic principles are introduced here that apply in every culture, in every situation where creation of understanding is the desire. The principles may be applied differently in the city as compared to rural areas, but the same dynamics are present. As you read, think how they can be applied among the people for which you have concern.

My prayer is that courageous friends living and working far from their homes, or even in their own neighborhood, will find greater satisfaction in their chosen service because they're learning to "make haste slowly."

Take time to learn before presuming to teach. Read…but go on to practice what you read!

Chapter Three

The Purpose Is Understanding

How can we communicate to benefit the people we want to help?

The first step is to know the proper goal of communication.

It's common to use communication selfishly, simply to meet our own goals, meeting our needs and perhaps our ideas about other people's needs. But when we communicate to achieve understanding, we help others gain the ability to meet their own needs, to solve their own problems. Without such understanding, communication skill too often leads to abusing people rather than strengthening them.

In Pavlov's well-known experiments he trained a dog to salivate upon hearing a bell. Sometimes we act as if we create spirituality the same way. We ring a church bell, and a man is expected to feel ready to sing and pray. *So this,* we may think, *is Christian communication?*

A Christian broadcaster wondered aloud, "Why can't we sell the gospel more effectively with radio?" He continued, "We can sell soap and we can sell tickets to entertainment. Why can't we sell the gospel?" Well, our purpose is not to "sell" the gospel. There's a qualitative difference between buying a product and committing one's whole self to Jesus Christ!

There's a similar difference when initiating change in any group. It's easy to forget that we're not simply trying to get people to do what they ought to do. That isn't development; it's control over other people. It's manipulation, and no one has the right to control another's life. We're *all* created in the image of God.

Development first requires understanding. And the value of communication arts is to develop mutual understanding. Let's examine parts of the ongoing process of communication so we can more effectively use its potential.

Communication, simply and incompletely described, involves three steps—perception, interpretation, and response.

Functional perception is the physical reception of the message, with the ears, eyes, all five of the senses. We detect the sounds, sights, smells, tastes, and touches that come to us. Those signals are transmitted from the sensory organs (eyes, ears, etc.) to the brain. Functional perception is the bare beginning of communication.

Interpretation involves the brain's structural perception as applied to the signals. It's this activity of the mind that develops meaning and understanding.

This two-step process—receiving signals and interpreting them—is the mechanism of understanding.

The third step—*response*—begins invisibly within the person's mind and core (heart), as understanding is developed by the receiver of communication. Though that understanding is unseen, it determines response. From that visible response, we can infer what understanding has been achieved.

From this simple summary of the communication process, it's evident that effective communication is not merely throwing a message at someone's eyes and ears. Even tossing it skillfully is still just throwing it. Bombardment of a stronghold in a war doesn't guarantee access to the stronghold unless the fort is destroyed and the occupants crushed. Neither does bombardment of a mind guarantee access to that mind, unless the individual's will is shattered by using methods such as brainwashing. This certainly is not development or evangelism, yet it may happen unintentionally because of great power carelessly used.

Governments, development and relief agencies, and mission groups often possess the power of technology, of economics, and of knowledge. That power can unintentionally crush people and force them to do what these outside groups wish. Simply having "agreeable" followers doesn't prove agreement or understanding. The reliable evidence is what happens when outside agencies leave. Too often, everything goes back to the way it was before the outsiders came.

During British rule of what is today the nation of South Sudan, the people produced some of the finest cotton in the world—having been forced to grow it through a system of laws and taxation. As a Sudanese leader explained, "We saw that it helped us. But when the British left, we stopped growing cotton! We had been compelled, so we made our choice *not* to grow cotton, even though it was against our own best interests!"

"Our people are like the weeping willow tree," explained another African church leader. "The wind may blow fiercely, but when it stops, the flexible branches go right back to where they were before the wind came." Winds of change often change nothing fundamentally.

Aid programs, development plans, even government programs have resulted in few lasting changes even in poor and oppressed communities where change is desperately needed. This is due not simply to temporarily accommodating pressure. It's largely the result of the way outsiders have approached change. Change is attempted by the use of power, rather than by creating understanding.

Change and development is first and fundamentally the development of people, as Tanzania's Julius Nyerere reminded us. Plans and programs may help by providing a way to interact. But they may also sidetrack effort by directing attention to questions of efficiency, technology, and money instead of to the questions of people. It's too easy to forget that attitudes are more important than techniques.

Reaching program goals can easily become more important than helping individuals. If there's conflict between individual needs and predetermined goals, the goals often come first. But the initial goal in any type of change must be to build understanding—understanding the insiders within their own world view, then helping them understand the outsiders who've come with the desire to help.

In the Scriptures, the word *understanding* is frequently used in relation to the most difficult change of all, change in the inner man. "A man of understanding," Solomon observes, "keeps a straight course" (Proverbs 15:21). In Psalm 119:144, the writer lays down a fundamental principle: "Give me understanding and I shall live." And Jeremiah 3:15 gives God's promise to His people: "I will give you pastors according to my heart who will guide you with wisdom and understanding." In numerous other references, understanding is shown to be essential to the fruitful life and to fruitful interaction with others.

Without understanding, no permanent change will result—even from the best intentions or the most powerful agencies. Instead of understanding, resentment slowly builds and may erupt to the surprise and chagrin of the outsider. We must first gain understanding of the people with whom we work as well as of the tasks we attempt. Then we must build understanding between ourselves and the people, so that desirable changes are shared goals.

Chapter Four

Meaning Cannot Be Transferred

When a brief description of an animal is read aloud to a group of four people, who then are instructed to draw it, they're likely to depict four different animals. The difference is primarily due not to their varying artistic skills, but to what they've experienced in the past.

Four people were asked to draw an animal that is furry, has a long tail, two ears, four legs, and a pointed nose. Here

are the pictures they drew:

How can the great differences be explained? All four people heard the same description. Yet one drew a mouse, another seems to have drawn a hyena, and another a rat. And the fourth creature? It's hard to name!

Each person puts his own meaning on what is said, not necessarily even understanding the meaning held by the person who gave the instructions. So we find four different pictures which illustrate four different meanings gained from the very same words, given at the same time.

Of course, if more *information*[1] is given, the meaning gained by each of the four persons will be more similar to each other. When that additional information is not given, we try to fill it in ourselves. We understand what we see, hear, smell, taste, or feel in wholes, not parts. If the whole isn't given, we unconsciously try to complete it.

If we see a fragment of paper, our mind tries to relate it to a whole paper. "Ah," we think, "This is part of a newspaper." Or when we hear a few notes of music, we fit those few notes into a whole. "That sounds like Chopin," or, "It reminds me of a folk song from India."

All signals that we perceive are related to a whole experience. Fragments that don't relate to anything else we've experienced are usually forgotten, though sometimes they worry us for hours or days until they can be identified. Identifying them is a matter of relating them to the "whole" that we already have in our memories. The accuracy of the meaning developed (that is, our meaning compared to the intended meaning) will depend upon the amount of information we have and how it relates to our previous experience.

This leads us to a very important basic proposition of communication: *Meaning cannot be transferred.* We can transfer information, but not meaning. Meaning is personal and can never be fully shared by anyone else. Meaning is always internal, hidden in the mind and existing nowhere else. Meaning is not a package that can be transferred from one person to another.

Teachers and preachers frequently say they'll "give the meaning" as they speak. Correctly speaking, that cannot be done because of the individual nature of meaning. Each individual creates the meaning within himself on the basis of the information received and the individual's previous experience.

The opportunities for misunderstanding are plentiful! When experience and previous knowledge are sharply different, highly diverse meanings will be gained from the same information and the same situation.

Consider the problem of good communication in medical, agricultural, or evangelistic programs. Think how difficult it is for the Acholi, or the Afghan, or the Argentine to develop the intended meaning when a Norwegian, Kenyan, or American speaks! How can the same meaning possibly be formed by both parties? The meaning cannot be given; that's impossible. What can be done is to transfer adequate information, so that similar meanings can be developed.

Teaching people of another culture is understandably difficult. As a result, the teacher from outside often has a low opinion of students of another culture. Comments like these are made: "I told them as simply and clearly as I could, and they just didn't understand. I don't think these people are very intelligent."

Meanwhile, what do you think those students say about the teacher? "He doesn't seem to understand how to behave properly." The insiders shake their heads in amazement. "This outsider isn't very bright. We've tried to explain to him, and he didn't understand a thing!"

Many misunderstandings arise because of different meanings for the same things. There's too little sharing of information—knowledge shared by insider and outsider, adding new "bits" so accurate meanings are developed.

Meaning is always constructed individually. When this is forgotten, it's too easy to describe other people with critical words: "All Poles are slow thinkers," or "All Americans are loud and arrogant." We assign incorrect meaning, then act on that meaning. The result is misunderstanding and resentment. The problem is caused by a very simple thing:

not acquiring enough information. Then, because of differing backgrounds, differing meanings are given to the same events.

The diagram here may aid understanding how communication functions. A sign is perceived, triggering an internal mental choice of model, which stimulates a thought, and a response is given—another sign. The middle parts of the process are invisible and internal, while the signs at the beginning and end are outward and apparent.

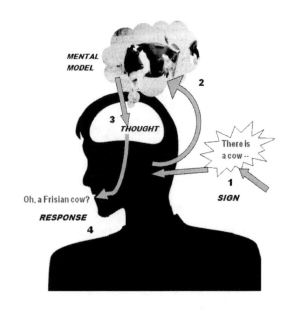

When interacting, enough information must be given to enable listeners to form a meaning close to that intended by the teacher. If incomplete information is given, the listener will interpret it according to his background, developing a meaning often very different from the teacher's intention. But this isn't a question of basic mental ability of the student. It's a question of different experience, different knowledge, and different assumptions. Cross-cultural communication often requires more information to be transferred because of these great differences in background.

Those who want to instruct others must learn to understand their experiences and the ideas (models) held in listeners' minds. Teaching can then be related to what's already understood by the students rather than to ideas held in the teacher's mind.

A model is a mental picture. It's our view of what things are like and how they're organized.

To illustrate, I draw a line:

As I continue to draw, I give you more information about the model, the mental picture, I have in mind.

Ah! You think I'm drawing the letter A, and that I'll finish by drawing the crossbar.

But then I give more information by extending the lines at the top, and drawing a smaller shape at the bottom. I'm again giving more information about the model I have in my mind.

At some point you suddenly grasp what I'm drawing—an American Indian tepee.

Your mental model is now similar to my mental model because I've given enough information for you to build your own mental model of a tepee. You've previously seen a tepee or a picture of one, so that experience is used in creating your own meaning. We have communicated, at least partially.

However, if you'd never seen a picture of a tepee, and had no experience with one, you couldn't build a mental model similar to mine. So there would be no effective communication.

When a sign is perceived—a word, a sound, a picture—it's always related to a mental model. The mental model depends upon previous experience, which is personal and individual. It also depends upon the environment. When you say "dry" while standing in a desert, it's a very different thing from saying "dry" while standing in a tropical rain forest. The environment itself conditions the model we have in our minds.

Obviously, the culture is involved. The culture tells you what you're supposed to see and how to handle it. Then there's the referent, the object itself. For example, when I say "stick," I'm referring to a specific object. If you can see the stick I'm talking about, we'll share the same referent. If you cannot see my stick, your experience and memory of sticks will become your referent—different now than my referent.

All these things form the models in our minds. These models are subject to continuing modification as new information comes. When a sign comes to our ears or our eyes, we say in effect, "Ah! Yes!" and then relate it to a specific model. That determines our response. If I say "cold," we'll each understand in terms of our culture environment, and relating that word to an existing mental model. We'll respond according to the information in that model.

It's obvious that the teacher must know what mental models are held in the pupil's mind. If he doesn't know this, he won't be able to relate new information to those existing models. As a result, what's taught will not be remembered, or will be completely misunderstood. What's heard may not even be similar to what is said.

When a person is told "crop rotation," does he have any idea of the subject being discussed? To what mental model does he relate "crop rotation"? Has he seen it tried and fail? Or does he think of a man who succeeded with it? When he's told to "use fertilizer," does he think of a man who succeeded, or a man who is called a witch because his crops were better than his neighbors? For a poverty-stricken family living in an urban slum, what meaning would be given to the terms *bank, savings,* and *security?* What does the phrase "high rise" mean to someone who has seen only small rural villages? Or consider some of the differences in meaning given to basic theological words such as *sin, incarnation, cross,* and *eternal life.*

Effective communication is not possible unless there's understanding of the mental model held by the person to whom you're communicating. This is fundamental in communication.

The only way to understand the mental models of the people is to be involved with the people. No book could be written to accurately describe all the mental models of a people, though ideas and suggestions could be gained from someone else's study. To communicate with the Didinga, the communicator must learn enough of their experiences, environment, and culture to understand the mental models held by the Didinga. Then the communicator can concentrate on giving more of the right kind of information to create understanding.

A number of factors determine which model is used—the environment, psychological needs at that time, knowing the thing referred to (referent), and the receiver's previous experience.

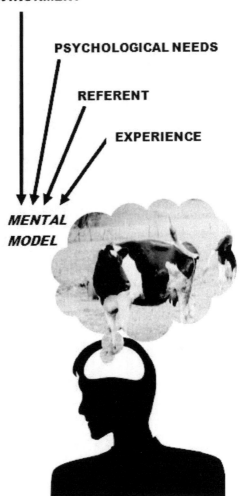

ENVIRONMENT

PSYCHOLOGICAL NEEDS

REFERENT

EXPERIENCE

MENTAL MODEL

When the images (mental models) in people's minds aren't known, real problems may arise. A government official in a small Ethiopian town was always well-dressed. Regardless of the time of the year, no matter how dusty or muddy the roads he traveled, this man was neat. Since it was important to the missionary living there to keep good relationships with this official, the missionary complimented him on three or four occasions, "My, that's a very smart looking suit. You always are well dressed, no matter what time of day."

Then one day the government official exploded with anger, "Why are you always accusing me of taking bribes?"

The missionary was hurt and puzzled, so he inquired from friends, "What did I say that made the official think I was accusing him of taking bribes?"

As he talked with friends he discovered that the official's mental model caused him to hear this meaning: "You're well dressed and neat out in this rural area of Ethiopia, so you must be 'eating the people.'" In other words, the missionary was accusing the official of taking bribes from the people in order to pay for his fine clothes! The government official heard an accusation, when the missionary meant to praise him—because the mental models of the two men were totally different. As a result, the missionary was never able to rebuild proper relationships with that particular official.

Even when we know what mental model other people hold, we may carelessly forget. We've learned new things, forgetting that other people haven't learned those things. The result is misunderstanding and strained relationships.

A Kenyan man went to America to study, and there he married an American girl. He came back to Kenya secure in a happy marriage. When some of his Kenyan friends visited him, he was delighted to see them. While he and his American wife were visiting with their guests, he offered a cup of tea. Of course, they accepted. So he went to the kitchen to make the tea while the wife remained to become better acquainted with his friends. The friends were so offended that they excused themselves and left before the tea came.

In an African home, a man does not prepare tea or food for visitors. That would show that he's totally dominated by the wife, that he's not a proper man. But in America, when the man helps with entertaining, as in making tea, it's a way to express love and respect for his wife. The Kenyan had learned the American way, but he used it at the wrong time, and the Kenyans were offended that the man was going to serve them tea. So they refused. The same signal was interpreted in two very different ways.

Different mental models can cause problems, some of them far more serious than a misunderstanding over a cup of tea. Those problems can be avoided only by careful listening and careful observing. Two simple words put into action can begin the creation of understanding between people of different cultures—*watch* and *imitate*. In other words, follow the examples of the host people. Carefully ask for customs to be explained to you, showing respect for their ways.

Chapter Five

Perfectly Logical

What has happened in this drawing?

"Well," you reply, "the character on the left shot the one on the right!"

That answer seems correct. But did you see the bullet? Did you see the gun actually fire? How do you know that the man on the right has only an arthritic elbow? Or isn't it possible that he shot himself, then the other man took the gun away from him?

On the basis of pictured evidence alone, no positive statement can be made.

The puzzle of what happened will be solved according to certain rules of logic. Some of those rules are part of cultural patterns. Others are learned during training in the laws of evidence or the rules of cause and effect. These rules control thinking so that sometimes evidence is assumed that isn't there. In other cases, information is blocked out because it seems irrelevant and illogical.

Logic, however, is not the same everywhere. It differs from culture to culture. "Logic" is not a fixed way of thinking that's universally accepted as correct. What is considered to be "logical" is built deeply into language and social relationships, so deeply in fact that each person assumes his kind of logic is universal. We assume that everybody follows what is good logic, if they're intelligent and acting reasonably. But then we meet people from another culture who don't follow the same logic. How do we react? Some say, "They aren't intelligent. They're confusing the issue. Are they even capable of real progress?" Because "they" don't follow "our" rules of logic, they're dismissed as incompetent. Emotional barriers begin to rise, and mutual understanding is almost impossible.

There are at least five different systems of logic followed in the world: linear, contextual, Semitic, Oriental, and Romance.[2] In Western cultures, linear logic is often considered the only logic. Contextual logic is considered "illogical"—rambling, disorganized, and inefficient. On the other hand, in many African and Asian societies, contextual logic is considered complete and the only reasonable way to approach a problem. Linear logic is considered sterile and disdainful of human values.

Look again at the picture of the two men. Usually the Westerner will be concerned here with two questions: 1) What happened? and 2) Who did it?   The illustration seems to make the answers to both questions quite clear. The cause

LINEAR LOGIC

is there—a smoking gun. Likewise we see the effect—a man presumably in pain, holding his elbow. This is a linear way of thinking, assuming a direct cause and effect relationship.

Linear Logic

Court cases in Western cultures are based on strong rules of evidence. The main prosecution and defense efforts are to find evidence directly related to the case. There's much legal argument about what evidence can be considered. The judge has the responsibility of deciding what is relevant and what is irrelevant. In effect, he draws a box around the case (like a frame around the illustration of the gun-pointing man and the elbow-holding man) and says that anything outside that box is irrelevant. If no direct relationship to the case "inside the box" can be established, the evidence isn't allowed. Introducing these "irrelevancies" is considered to confuse the issue of deciding what happened, who did it, and fixing punishment.

Contextual Logic

A person raised to think in a contextual manner is much more likely to ask a different question: "Why did he do it?" He would look at the reason for the happening, the relationships of the people involved, and try to understand the total surroundings or context of the event. What personal pressures are these two characters experiencing? What's the

weather like, and how good are their relationships with other people in the group?

Because the emphasis here is on examining an event in its total context, this is called contextual logic. Unfortunately, this approach is not even considered logic in most Western cultures. It's thought to be too emotional, confusing the issues rather than helping us understand what happened.

In traditional courts of Africa, on the other hand, thorough discussion of the context of the incident is encouraged. The emphasis is to understand why it happened and how to restore balance in disturbed relationships. A conclusion is reached slowly, to allow ample time to consider everything surrounding the case.

If cows walk into a neighbor's garden and begins eating the crops, linear logic will ask, "Where's the herd boy responsible for those cows? Why isn't he doing his job? It's his fault that the cows are in the neighbor's garden." But the traditional African court of inquiry will probably not ask such things. Knowing who's responsible, they'll more likely ask, "Why did the cows go into that particular garden? Why did they go into any garden at all? What moved the cows to act in that way?"

Such a "simple" case would take perhaps fifteen minutes in most Western courts, with the purpose being to fix responsibility and then to penalize the one who failed in his duty. But similar discussions can easily last half a day in traditional African courts. The traditional courts seek to understand why the cows went into the garden, and then find the best way to restore "balance" in the society. How can the man whose garden was damaged be compensated?

The herd boy is not usually punished, though he may have been away catching a field mouse and roasting it over a fire. Why punish him for doing what boys do? That's not a surprising way to act. What's important is to find out what caused the cow to act in that way. Then good relationships must be restored between the owners of the cow and the owners of the garden, so there won't be growing anger in the community.

The differences between linear and contextual logic originate in the differences between what's considered important in various cultures. For example, in African cultures it's extremely important to maintain proper relationships between people and between people and their environment. Consequently, African use of logic tends to be for the purpose of restoring balance in a disturbed situation. This must involve the total context, not merely a narrow part that would fix blame. So a very wide range of information may be considered "evidence" in seeking to solve a problem.

The Westerner would consider much information used in contextual logic as irrelevant and distracting. He seeks a direct and identifiable relationship between an effect and its causes. If something cannot be shown as part of a chain of cause, it's useless information and so discarded. The Westerner's primary purpose is not to restore social and spiritual balance, but to fix blame. So his "rules of evidence" are different in order to achieve different purposes. The difference goes back to the very core of culture where different assumptions are held about what is real and what is important.

How does contextual logic function in international matters? During the 1976 Olympic Games in Montreal, the African and Asian athletic teams went there ready to participate. However, instead of competing, their governments instructed them to boycott the games because Olympic authorities had refused to ban New Zealand teams from the games. The Afro-Asian athletes would have had to compete with New Zealanders, who had competed with South Africa in rugby. Rugby is not an Olympic sport. The real target of the boycott was South Africa (which was not allowed to compete in the Olympics), because their racial policies discriminated against Africans and Asians. Since New Zealand had competed against South Africa, they were seen as giving encouragement to South Africa to continue its policies. Thus, a boycott of the Olympics.

On a simple scale of 1 to 5, with 1 representing "logical" and 5 "illogical," how is the logic of that decision rated? When mature African church leaders rated the decision, as well as missionaries from Great Britain and the United States, all Africans rated it at 2, moderately logical. All the Americans and British rated the decision at either 4 or 5, moderately or entirely illogical.

For the Africans, the decision was logical because the various parts of life (sports, religion, politics) cannot be separated. It's logical to do something in one area of life in order to have an effect in other areas. Since many of the African countries had world champions, they hoped to draw attention to the problem by withdrawing from the competition in protest. This approach to a problem was irrelevant by Western linear logic, but highly relevant by contextual logic.

British and Americans considered it illogical because sports are separate from political matters. Little or no relationship is seen between how a man performs in sports and the rightness or wrongness of his politics. For the Westerner who thinks in terms of rules of evidence, the Olympics in Montreal were "outside the box" within which evidence could be applied to the problem of South Africa's racial policies.

Contextual Logic in the Bible

The Bible has examples of both contextual and linear logic. For example, the book of Romans is a classic example of linear thinking. Paul builds an argument point by point, concluding each one with a "therefore." One subject leads directly to the next, making it relatively easy for the

Westerner to outline the book and follow the pattern of thinking.

In contrast, the book of Hebrews is structured contextually. The dominant focus of Hebrews is the supremacy of Jesus Christ. First, His supremacy in relation to the traditions of the ancestors is brought out. Next, Christ's supremacy to the Lord's messengers (angels) is introduced, followed by Christ's supremacy as the final sacrifice, as the great high priest, and as the One who can give help.

Westerners frequently have difficulty with Hebrews because it isn't linear and not easily boxed into an outline or a series of statements with a conclusion. It instead examines one topic from a series of perspectives. When these separate topics are put together, the basis for much of Christian theology is given. Both Romans and Hebrews center on the supremacy of Christ over all things, but show His supremacy using different styles of logic.

The use of parables illustrates contextual logic. They don't teach by propositions, but by showing a slice of life. Teaching is seen in its true context, as a part of everyday life. The use of allegories and traditional stories is very similar. Learning occurs by way of stories, rather than by a series of statements.

Contextual logic includes the relationships involved in a particular event, so the total setting is considered. It's wrong to think of contextual thinking as either logical or illogical; it's simply different. The person who thinks contextually views life as a whole rather than a series of parts. He sees the threads of life knotted together, rather than making up a chain.

This approach to thinking even affects the usage of time. The linear thinker views time as something happening in sequence. He's concerned with the accurate chronology of events. This event happened first, then the next event was this, and so on to the end of the story.

The man who thinks contextually is much more likely to look at events themselves as important, rather than the order in which they happened. Events mark his people's history, and are the way by which birth and death are remembered. Between notable events, time is measured primarily in the annual cycle of planting and harvesting. The annual cycle stimulates contextual thinking, since it's circular rather than linear.

The strength of linear logic is in the ability to determine cause and effect. On that pattern, a technology has developed that can modify the environment and magnify human minds and strength. Since the West values technology, Westerners of course believe that linear thinking is real logic; thus, all other kinds of thinking are illogical.

Even the Westerner, however, uses contextual thinking. But as he's more educated in Western tradition, his linearity of thinking increases. He comes to disregard contextual approaches. The same is true of Africans or Asians. As they're more educated in the Western linear model (dominant in the world today), they too become more linear in their approach to life.

Let's look closer now not only at linear and contextual logic, but also at the other three logic systems we've identified—Semitic, Oriental, and Romance.

Oriental Logic

A third form of logic, the Oriental, is perhaps best diagramed as circular. A matter is examined carefully from differing viewpoints, somewhat like a wrestler circling around his opponent looking for a place to attack, but never attacking. The "attack" is more by

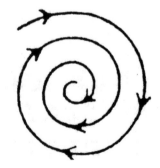

inference rather than a direct statement. Directness is a violation of courtesy. In a communication event, it's more courteous to leave the conclusion to the other participant.

For example, it's said that although there's a word for "no" in Japanese, it's so seldom used that outsiders wonder if it exists. A negative answer is understood by the manner in which "yes" is spoken or suggested. Needless to say, this style of logic and interaction is frustrating to the more direct Westerner!

Again, there are biblical examples of this approach, notably in the four gospels, Matthew, Mark, Luke, and John. Jesus shows by His actions and parables that He is God. He says that He is the Bread of Life, the Living Water, the Good Shepherd, the Light of the World, and conveys other aspects of His nature that could mean only that He is God. He says He is one with the Father, God Himself, who sent Him. And His hearers understand what He's saying—though He does not directly state, "I am God." A clear statement of His divinity is left for one of His disciples to give: "We believe and know that you are the Holy One of God" (John 6:69).

Modern Japan is one example of the combination of a linear/technological and an Oriental (contextual) approach to life. Japanese engineers demonstrate their ability to use a linear approach to problems. But employers more often follow an Oriental approach in administration of their companies. When an employee is hired, his whole life is taken into consideration—retirement, provision for education, social events, travel, etc. The company hiring him becomes a "family" for him. He's not divided into parts, one part for work on the assembly line, one part a community member, and one part in religious activity. The company becomes his total context, and that controls his approach to all of life.

Semitic Logic

A fourth distinctive pattern of logic has been called Semitic, and is most frequently observed in Middle Eastern societies. This style of logic in communication proceeds part way in a story or problem, then goes back to repeat the latter part of what was just presented before carrying the story further forward. In a long story this pattern is repeated several times, somewhat like shingles laid on a roof—the overlapping makes certain that the whole story holds together in the listeners' memories, to accomplish its purpose. It's particularly suited to oral communication. The form may be used not only for individual accounts, but also for long histories of a community or a people, both oral and written.

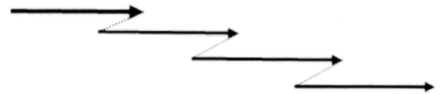

The Hebrews, a Semitic people, often used this form. The historical books of the Hebrew Scriptures follow this pattern, as does the Genesis account of beginnings in chapters one and two. Hebrew poetry also reflects this overlapping pattern of presentation, as demonstrated in the opening lines of Psalm 38:

> O LORD, do not rebuke me in your anger
> or discipline me in your wrath.
> For your arrows have pierced me,
> and your hand has come down upon me.

A statement is made, then the next line restates the same thought, adding different or amplified phrases, carrying the argument further toward the major point.

In John 6:25-69, the Semitic pattern is followed by Jesus as He leads the crowd to understand that He Himself is the Bread of life. He first directs their thinking away from the miraculous feeding of 5,000 men to the "food that endures to eternal life." (6:27) He takes them a step further by suggesting that the desired food is "to believe in the one he has sent." Then Jesus corrects their idea that Moses gave the manna in the wilderness, reminding them that "my Father...gives the true bread from heaven." (6:32). His next statement is the summation of what had been said: "I am the Bread of life." Jesus continued teaching in this manner within the crowd's logic style to lead them to comprehension of the truth He was giving. They understood, and the issue remaining was unavoidable—to reject Him, or to believe and follow Him.

Romance Logic

A fifth suggested pattern of logic has been labeled as Romance. It's widely used in daily life particularly among cultures using one of the Romance languages. It is not used exclusively; though it's the dominant pattern in some

cultures, one or more of the other logic patterns may at times be used by various group members. That's also true, of course, in all cultures; a dominant logic is not the *only* pattern followed.

Romance logic has been described as emotionally driven. Choices are made on the basis of how one feels, after perhaps a quick summary of available facts about alternatives.

A young, talented couple lived in a culture where Romance logic dominated, in a country where a brutal, oppressive regime was in control. When the opportunity arose, they fled the country, but in doing so they were forced to leave behind their daughter, their only child. They felt this was their only chance at freedom; later, they reasoned, they could find a way to get their daughter out as well. Meanwhile, she was cared for by grandparents. The parents were distressed over the separation, and sought help in many places—schools they attended, churches that prayed for their country, and political figures. Repeatedly they were told that there was no way to bring out their daughter; political realities and legal barriers prevented it.

For more than a decade, they had no success. Only after thirteen years, during which the little child they left had become a young woman, were they reunited.

The couple had been desperate for freedom, leading them to listen to ill-informed people and to follow advice that "felt" encouraging. Emotion dominated their thinking, unseasoned by the facts.

Those in cultures driven by Romance logic know that facts are important, but if feelings disagree with facts, the facts are often ignored. The husband of the couple mentioned above was a medical doctor, trained to observe facts and make his diagnosis on the basis of those facts. But emotion dominated in a critical life decision. A safer conclusion would have been sustained by facts, not only by emotion.

Logic and Faith

Where does faith enter into our logic patterns?

There are times when we believe something is right or wrong; even when all the facts aren't available, we make a decision based on our faith. Though it seems to go against common judgment, in reality it depends on the adequacy of whom we trust. When the one we trust has given directions, we can be confident in the decision even when all facts are not perceived.

How do these differences in thinking affect the way we communicate?

In cultures dominated by linear logic, the Christian message is predominantly expressed in reasoned discourses and sermons that are careful outlines of biblical truth. The life of Jesus is explained in carefully reasoned essays and books, showing who He is and how we should respond to Him. An excellent example of this is in Timothy Keller's writings, geared to the audiences of New York City's professional class.[3]

The same truth is expressed in the beauty of Orthodox ritual and places of worship, but appealing primarily to emotion through the senses. Art, architecture, and worshipful reenactment of the essence of the gospel are dominant in cultures where Romance logic is most common.

Contextual logic gives high value to interpersonal relationships and the participation of the spirit world in human life, while giving less value to visible cause and effect patterns. The result is often a two-level form of Christianity, with the linear form from the West visible and belief in spirits largely invisible, reserved for times of crisis. In large societies where face-to-face relationships can include only part of the people, linear communication and thinking become more common. Strong print media emerges, extending the number that can hear the message. By the very nature of print media, thinking is molded into linear patterns. The nature of mass media, with only limited audience participation possible, favors one-way, linear communication.[4]

In linear logic, the emphasis is on cause and effect, casting aside anything not related to that primary relationship. Emotional values tend to be lost as a result.

In contextual logic, events are the primary time orientation instead of the sequence and chronology that are important in linear thinking.

Semitic logic is well-suited to a society that's primarily oral, where very strong value is given to accuracy of remembering group history and values.

In pointing out differences in logics, it's easy to forget that no group is completely one or the other. If we could position patterns of thought on a line, each group could be placed at some point on that line. Western societies would usually be nearer the linear end of the line, and Asian groups nearer the contextual, Semitic, and Oriental end of the line.

No group or person is totally linear or totally contextual in thinking. The value in recognizing these different patterns is to develop the ability to work within the dominant thought patterns of the people with whom we seek to build communication, seeing both strengths and weaknesses

Linear logic is misused when it excludes everything except the immediately relevant. It greatly limits our understanding of the world and of God. Reducing the world to a series of laws and propositions explains much, some would dare to say everything. But after all, the world is a tiny place compared to the whole universe. Even if linear logic could give us explanations of everything in the world, could that be extended to the whole universe? Could it go beyond and explain the infinite—God Himself? Any attempt to confine God to the box of our reasoning will fail. Infinity cannot be put into a finite box. In the attempt we lose not only total comprehension, but also nonlinear things like beauty, joy, and peace.

§

I tried to understand God

by breaking Him up

and straightening tangled lines

into clear patterns.

I got Him sorted out into neat parts

with their own places and boundary lines,

and God started to get lost.

(Sana Anderson)[5]

PART TWO

Paying the Price to Begin Change

To this point, we've glimpsed the challenges of intercultural communication. Our fundamental purpose is to create understanding of the particular Message we bring, and with understanding, to see people changed. That all seems impossibly naïve! Other people not only act and speak differently, but also perceive and think differently.

Where do we begin? With a visit? A program? Or a new organization? None of those easy actions are an answer.

You must begin with the people themselves, in a way that's costly beyond expectation. You must give up your life.

Jesus said it most clearly, comparing us to grains of wheat: "Unless a kernel of wheat falls to the ground and dies, it remains only a single seed. But if it dies, it produces many seeds" (John 12:24).

That's the price of embedding the Message in other lives.

Chapter Six

Communication Is Involvement

How can I possibly learn so much about people from a different culture, with different ideas and different needs than my own?

Only by listening, observing, asking questions, taking part in community affairs, and entertaining and being entertained by the people you're trying to know. Laugh and cry with them, enjoy their good times, and grieve with them when there's grief in the community.

Romans 12:14-16 directs the Christian not only to be involved within the culture of others, but to humbly accept both pleasant and hurtful reactions:

> Bless those who persecute you; bless and do not curse. *Rejoice with those who rejoice; mourn with those who mourn.* Live in harmony with one another. Do not be proud, but be willing to associate with people of low position. Do not be conceited.

The book of Ecclesiastes describes deep involvement with all of life, the kind of involvement necessary to enter deeply into the life of another people:

> There is a time for everything, and a season for every
> activity under heaven: a time to be born and a time to
> die, a time to plant and a time to uproot... a time to tear
> down and a time to build, a time to weep and a time to
> laugh, a time to mourn and a time to dance...a time to
> embrace and a time to refrain...a time to keep and a time
> to throw away, a time to tear and a time to mend, a time
> to be silent and a time to speak. (Ecclesiastes 3:1-7)

Our motive is to communicate—make known—the joy and grace that are in Jesus. That is accomplished by full involvement with those with whom we want to communicate. Thus the brief statement that is the foundation of all else: *Communication is involvement.*

Deceptively simple in its expression, this statement is difficult to live out in daily life. It's not a question of being involved in order to communicate; it's rather that involvement and communication are inseparable. *Without involvement there is no communication.* We communicate by being involved with people's lives. Even if it's not intentional giving of a message, your involvement *is* communication.

Sending and receiving messages can be very impersonal, a separate thing from real communication. Effective communication that creates understanding occurs only through involvement in each other's lives and interests. A supposedly ancient Chinese proverb goes like this: "Tell me, and I'll forget; show me, and I may remember; involve me, and I'll understand."

Involvement is not merely the beginning of communication; it's more like the water in which a fish swims. Without water the fish can neither swim nor survive. And without involvement, effective communication simply cannot occur.

Communication techniques can be used very skillfully without communicating. Communication includes not only the act of sending a message, but the achievement of understanding. How do we begin achieving that? We begin by establishing commonness.

There are several related words in English that help to illustrate the nature of communication:

> *community*—having in common the same geography or interest
>
> *commune*—sharing possessions and a way of life
>
> *communism*—an ideology that advocates common ownership, eliminating private property
>
> *communion*—sharing intimately, and especially applied to sharing in the life of Christ and of His body, the church
>
> *communicate*—the sharing of information and ideas to develop mutual understanding

All these words are formed from the Latin root *communis,* a word that carries the idea of "having in common" or "sharing in something."

Mutual understanding comes with interaction. A number of words in English refer to different aspects of "commonness." One is *reciprocity*—having a reciprocal relationship, or more simply, giving and taking from one another. Another common word is *correspondence*—co-response, or exchanging responses. The exchange of messages, experiences, attitudes, and thoughts builds the commonness essential for communication.

Too often we try to communicate without having anything in common. We try to transmit a message, but understanding isn't achieved because we do not have "commonness." The Malagasy language expresses an insight into the true nature of communication by using the same word for both involvement and communication, *fifandraisana.*

You do not have communication unless there's a large area of commonness where people's lives overlap, making possible the understanding of one another. If my life is totally separate from yours, I may send you a message and you may send a message back, but there'll be little understanding.

Obviously there must be commonness of language, yet more is needed. Unless there's commonness of experience, understanding does not occur. As you seek to communicate with Acholi, Lotuho, Russian, or Czech, where's the commonness? It's much easier to be with people from your own country. With them, you have large areas of commonness. You remember similar experiences and ideas, and you have similar needs. Understandably, everyone looks forward to being together.

Conversely, trying to communicate outside your own countrymen is considerably more difficult. The experience of trying to communicate with someone with whom you have little in common is stressful. You need to first develop commonness through involvement; otherwise the situation becomes intolerable. You'll run, not walk, to someone with whom you can communicate! We all need communication and understanding for good mental health.

To a greater or lesser degree, we're all in the situation of trying to communicate with people where there's little commonness. You'll create understanding and stimulate development to the degree you're able to establish commonness. If you can't establish commonness, you cannot communicate.

Communication is frequently confused with mere transmission. Transmission acts as if programs and tools do the communicating. However, a program to tell the people of a new seed or a new treatment for a disease may not communicate at all. Or if we have useful new tools such as tape cassettes or full-color posters, we may think we're communicating when we use these things, yet they're never adequate if involvement is lacking.

"How well you talk! I feel quite drowsy, it is just like being in church." So wrote A. A. Milne in *Winnie the Pooh*. Many times we assume that communication occurs because everything is done so well. But like too many church services, there's no involvement, and thus only apparent and superficial communication.

Involvement will develop in four stages: 1) developing common languages, 2) developing common experiences, 3) participating in common cultural patterns, and 4) understanding or sharing basic assumptions.

Developing Common Languages

A first step to involvement is developing the ability to understand all languages of that particular culture. In Chapters 8 and 9, all these languages of culture will be introduced. The verbal language is important; however in many situations it's not as important in achieving understanding as most or all the other eleven languages, each with their own local variations. English, French, Spanish, Hindi, or Mandarin are widely used, even internationally, and may be useful in trade and national government. When your calling compels you to be involved deeply in the lives of people, it's necessary to acquire the verbal language of friendship and family. The bulk of the person's life cannot be touched, nor real understanding achieved, until the home language is used.

Outside the home, the serious issues of change, of development, and of the Christian message demand use of the home language. Involvement with people demands common languages, and the degree of language sharing will determine the depth of involvement.

Developing Common Experiences

The second step toward involvement is sharing common experience. Without common experiences, how can issues of change be shared? Common experience is a necessity. The difficulty is that outsiders have very little experience in common with most of the people where they're working. They've seldom slept overnight in the homes of the people, or shared a meal there. They haven't had the experience of knowing that a crop must survive or they die. It is seen intellectually, even with some emotion; that's not the same as living constantly with those realities.

How can that shortcoming be overcome? It's difficult to share the experiences of people in another culture, but common ground must be developed. It isn't suggested that we live exactly as the people live, abandoning our own identities, though sometimes that's necessary. There's a strong argument for modeling alternative lifestyles in a way that the local people can replicate within their resources and technical skills. While the outsider's lifestyle is different, it isn't so different as to seem strange, foreign, and unattainable.

It's not involvement in a program that matters, but involvement in lives. Programs are important, but they won't succeed unless there's communication. Communication doesn't succeed without involvement. Involvement depends upon common experiences.

I had a close Zimbabwean friend, now deceased. We traveled together, stayed together, and were in difficulties together. We've been stuck overnight on deep, muddy roads, and been in danger together. Even after several years of absence, this man remained a close friend. When we could again be together, immediately we sat down and talked easily about both small news and serious issues. We communicated within the framework of our common experiences.

In the 1970s, a number of Cambodian refugees were resettled in the United States. Since churches were helping in the resettlement, the Cambodians were brought to church services. These Cambodians spoke no English. Nobody in the church spoke Cambodian. Yet communication was established. The people in the church became involved with every aspect of the Cambodians' lives. They helped them learn ways of living in the community, yet retaining their own cultural identity. One family showed me Bible lessons they had prepared for the Cambodians.

I looked through the lessons with concern. The lessons seemed to assume that Cambodians were simply Americans who couldn't speak English. Cambodian traditions, their Buddhist religious assumptions, and their culture were ignored. What could I say that would help? Finally, rather weakly, I suggested, "The Cambodians will be very interested in learning I'm sure." And they were. They were very interested. The classes grew from five or six to fifty or more who came for the Bible lessons.

Why did they come? First of all, the Bible lessons were printed in Cambodian. Someone had been found to do the translation. The Cambodian was printed immediately below the English, translated directly word for word. With that direct, word-for-word translation, the Cambodian must hardly have made sense. Yet the people came. It gave them an opportunity to be closely involved with the American people where they were trying to build a new life. The Cambodians didn't understand what the Bible was all about; they did appreciate the Christian people who were willing to take the time to be with them, to be involved with them. A common experience was being shared, and that made the difference.

A deliberately planned shared experience from Germany was reported by a pastor there: "Pastors in the Evangelical Lutheran Church of Hanover exchanged their clerical garments for overalls to work for four weeks in factories in the area. At first our colleagues in the factories were surprised and amazed, but when they discovered that we had come not just to watch but to really work, they accepted us. Some workers had the opportunity to show the pastor that they could help him, how the work was done, or how the machines were operated. Later on these new workers, the pastors, were also asked to help with marital problems or deaths and the desperate attempts by foreigners to find places where they could live.

"Doors were opened that had seemed totally closed to the ministry of the gospel. Those who exchanged the pulpit for the assembly line know that for the bulk of the workers the church is hardly attractive. Only when you have experienced this can you be accepted by the workers as someone worth talking to."[6]

This is true not just in Germany, but everywhere. Teaching cannot begin until the learners feel that the teachers are part of their lives, showing that they're worth listening to. Training, skills, and money for training programs are not as important as sharing experiences.

Sharing Common Cultural Patterns

Deepening involvement comes by participating in common cultural patterns. It's not truly possible to share completely in another culture. Still, there are certain parts, certain cultural patterns that can be learned and shared.

For example, there's a Norwegian cultural pattern not followed among people in my home culture—fish for breakfast and fish for supper, twice a day, every day. In most American cultures, fish would be eaten only for dinner, and even that infrequently. The idea of putting fish on bread is surprising. Instead, fish is served hot on a plate, not cold on a piece of bread! Nonetheless, an American living with

Norwegians should learn to share this small cultural pattern of Norway as a start in practicing other cultural patterns.

In Sudan, work starts at six o'clock in the morning. That would be incredible in, say, northern Europe. Some people are scarcely waking up then, and most are still asleep. Work starts at eight, or at nine in many professional jobs. Conversely, in Sudan a half-day's work is finished by that time. Different people; different cultural patterns.

In India there's a culture that recognizes only six different times of the day. Each period of the day and night is named for the flower that opens at that time. They do not note smaller units of time.

For most Germans, a meeting announced for 7:15 will begin at 7:15 sharp! An Englishman would probably be there at 7:10 or 7:20, but not 7:15—which is too precise, too rigid for the cultural patterns with which he's most comfortable.

A meeting for traditional Zulus announced for seven o'clock would probably have enough people present to begin at about 7:30. They wouldn't want to come at seven, because that would imply they were pushy, dominant, and a little bit proud. Arriving about 7:30 indicates readiness to come and participate without trying to control. Lateness may well be a matter of politeness. If we're going to be involved with people following such patterns, we must participate in those patterns.

How many times has hurry destroyed relationships? A different cultural pattern in use of time has caused damage, even distrust of one another.

A foreign development worker may have gone to the home of an African colleague at the beginning of a trip. He hurried to the African coworker's home and called, "Let's go!" But to his dismay, the coworker is not at all prepared to depart. He doesn't have his things together, so he invites, "Well, come in and sit down."

Then the foreigner is served tea—when he wants to hurry out to begin the journey. He's so impatient! He wants to get on the way, but now they're taking time to drink a cup of tea! If this is a first visit to the home, not to drink or eat what is offered is considered an insult. This seems a small matter, yet it can cause great tension.

It's obvious that we cannot become what we are not. A Sudanese cannot become a Norwegian, nor can an American become a Kenyan. But it isn't necessary to become someone else to share in their cultural patterns. Those patterns can be learned, and must be entered into as part of effective communication.

Understanding Basic Assumptions

To become deeply involved with the host group, it's necessary to understand their basic assumptions about life, about the world, about human relationships, and about the supernatural. Basic assumptions are held at a deep level, almost sub-consciously. These are the things "known" to be true that aren't open to debate. Serious questioning of these assumptions causes confusion, resentment, and anger.

Perhaps the best way to understand the importance of basic assumptions is by example.

Agricultural demonstrators in the Transkei area of South Africa decided they would show the people the value of fertilizer. So they set up several demonstrations, in cooperation with a few farmers. They persuaded them to use fertilizer and see the difference. Indeed, as they used the fertilizer, the farmers had a greatly increased yield. The agricultural demonstrators were convinced that their demonstration had convinced the farmers to fertilize. But next year, no other farmers would use fertilizer. Even the demonstration farmers refused to use fertilizer.

The European agricultural demonstrators assumed that if something could be successfully demonstrated, everybody else would imitate it to share in the success. But this did not happen. In frustration, the agricultural demonstrators blamed the Transkei people: "The Natives are so conservative." All the usual words of frustration poured out: "They're stupid, they don't understand, they'll never change, they're ignorant." All because the farmers refused to follow the methods that had been demonstrated.

And of course the Transkei farmers had lots of words for the agricultural demonstrators! "They're proud, they're arrogant, they don't care about people's feelings, they're coming to exploit and oppress us." Neither group understood the other.

Eventually the demonstrators had to leave. The effort to improve productivity had failed.

Why this refusal by the farmers, after a "successful" demonstration of the benefits of fertilizer? The Transkei farmers considered that the European demonstrators had bewitched the land of neighboring farms so that all the goodness from the neighbor's land flowed into the demonstration plots. That was why their crop was good and the neighbor's crop was poor. The agricultural demonstrators had shown their ability to control the vital spirits of the land; clearly they were "witches" of a very high and powerful kind.

Understandably, the people feared to use fertilizer again, because if they continued growing better crops than their neighbors it would prove that they, too, were bewitching their neighbors. The penalty for being a witch in that culture was death.

The real problem was not a question of language. They shared both a language and much common experience—the demonstrators were also farmers from the same part of Africa. They even shared certain common cultural patterns. Nevertheless, there was a breakdown in understanding. What happened? Basic assumptions of the farmers and the demonstrators about the way the world works were wholly different. The learning of assumptions is a necessary foundation for communication.

Ideas about beauty—whether a landscape is beautiful or dull, whether flowers are more beautiful than cows, or the shimmering heat of a desert noon more appealing than the damp coolness of a green forest—are determined by basic assumptions about good and bad and even the nature of life itself. These assumptions control what we perceive. Less important things are simply ignored, and we're hardly even aware of them. Our basic assumptions determine what we see and to what we'll respond.

Only through involvement can basic assumptions of other groups be learned. Building a framework for communication moves from a common language, to the sharing of common experiences, into participating in common cultural patterns, and finally reaching the deepest level—understanding another's basic assumptions about life. Understanding someone else's basic assumptions doesn't mean we accept all of them. But if we understand them, we can learn to work together.

A Beginning in Application—Becoming Dependent

It's difficult to begin involvement with a different people. Frequently, the receptor group is suspicious of the outsider's intentions and unwilling to openly receive him into their inner society.

Genuine involvement can be established, however, when you're dependent on the host group. This sets to one side the issues of power, making possible the building of genuine understanding. That alternative may not exist where work is already begun. Perhaps then, dependency can be practical only in limited areas. But where possible, the trappings of power should be left behind. Then the host people will be able to maintain their feelings of self-worth and dignity. Who enjoys entertaining a long-term guest who has no need of the host's friendship, counsel, or even food and shelter? It should not be surprising when the host accuses the guest of exploitation.

The experience of Bruce Olson in becoming dependent on his hosts is reported in his book *Bruchko*.[7] Olson went to the Motilone Indians of South America as a missionary, depending totally upon them for food and survival. It was five years before he saw the gospel preached in the Motilone society. During those years he had learned the language and become part of their life. He nearly died twice, and the Motilone nursed him back to health. Then Olson's one convert in five years found the opportune time to tell the whole society of the gospel. The news of Christ spread overnight, like fire in dry grass. The whole society began to change, yet retaining significant aspects of their own culture.

The Motilone people, some fifteen years later, were among the most developed South American Indian people with clinics, schools, and self-government—all operated by themselves. The United Nations has asked Olson to talk before their committees regarding methods for helping so-called underdeveloped peoples. It's a fantastic story of suffering and success.

Development and mission agencies are rarely dependent upon anybody in the countries where they work, though help from outside is often needed. Little that can be offered locally is needed. It's impractical, and probably impossible, to now reverse operational styles. However, some degree of dependency is necessary to establish involvement. When we can become dependent upon the people (even in small ways), it sharply improves communication.

How Can So Few Become Involved with So Many?

It's an overwhelming task—to become involved with so many different people with so many desperate needs. How can one person, or one small group, become involved equally with the

Didinga, the Lotuho, the Toposa, and the Acholi? How can one become involved with so many?

It's impossible. One person can be significantly involved with only a few people. Some management theory reports that twelve people are the maximum number who can report directly to one overseer, and still succeed in working together as a reasonably close unit. The more ideal number is seven or eight.

With limited capacity for close involvement, what can be done?

Let's consider how the numbers add up. First, your family must have your closest involvement. We'll consider that to be three people. Then there are your immediate friends, perhaps two more people. Your fellow workers coming from your own culture probably involve at least four additional people. So you're already closely involved with nine people. But those nine don't all need to have close involvement with one another, so some room is left for you to include other people from outside those immediate groups.

Close involvement and friendship is probably possible with only three or four additional people. These "openings" will require your remaining time and emotional strength. And what is three or four with the tens of thousands that you desire to help? The only way that can be useful is by considering those three or four as "bridges"[8] into the host culture. By being closely involved with these few, the impact of your life and work can effectively spread throughout the whole community.

Intercultural communication is never easy, and represents a challenge to the common affliction of ethnocentrism. It begins with involvement, often personally costly. In the next chapters we identify the probable price of effective communication.

Chapter Seven

Using a Third Culture

Mission and development goals can be reached without turmoil and resentments, if the fundamental principle of communication is remembered and practiced— *communication is involvement.* When the messenger is deeply involved with the people to whom he brings the message, receiving and acting on the message is probable.

The outside messenger cannot become an insider, but through extensive involvement he can create commonness with the people to whom he brings change. He can become a meeting place between the two cultures. Some things and some experiences can be shared. Forms of language (*all* the languages of culture) can be learned that both insider and outsider understand and share.

In this sharing, we form new culture patterns. In effect, we form a *third culture* that's different from either the "first culture" of the inside group or the "second culture" of the messenger. This third culture shares common characteristics with both originating cultures.

In this third culture, there's opportunity for discussion and consideration of innovations. Matters can be discussed freely in the new friendships and loyalties of a third culture that would be difficult or even dangerous in either the first or second cultures. Deliberate use of a third culture strategy is an excellent way to introduce positive change.

To use this strategy effectively, we need to look closely at 1) how a third culture is formed, 2) what it is like, and 3) how to use it for change.

The third culture group is not usually large. It's not a formally structured group, but simply people who share many experiences and take part in many of the same activities. It's usually limited in its membership to people working on a common project and sharing common experiences. When these people are together, they enjoy each other's company because of the commonness they've built by living together in a new place or a new country, by working together on a difficult task, or by a similar bonding experience. They'll more readily listen to the suggestions coming from among themselves. There's a friendly warmth and good will that leads to trust between members.

Soldiers who have served together become members of a third culture that is distinct from the home cultures of the soldiers. When foreign missionaries were interned in prison camps during war in China, they developed a very close-knit culture that was different than the English, Swedish, American, Norwegian, Methodist, Baptist, Lutheran cultures from which they came. Those who had been opposed to each other became participants in this new culture where they could be friends—often to their mutual surprise.

More commonly, a successful sports team has developed an *esprit de corps,* strong bonds that lead to enjoyment and trust among them. Successful professional sports teams frequently have members from different national cultures— American, French, Spanish, Australian—and different religious beliefs. But they've built a common third culture centered on playing the game well and winning. Jokes are shared, along with concerns from outside the sport. The friendships formed often last a lifetime.

These third cultures are informal and often unplanned. They're not usually the result of conscious effort, but come from sharing within a setting that's new to all the participants. Yet there's little reason why a third culture cannot be deliberately planned, then used as a bridge into another culture, as illustrated here.

Though these two cultures are near each other in space, they share very little in common. But a third culture gives an

In a diagram it can be seen like this:

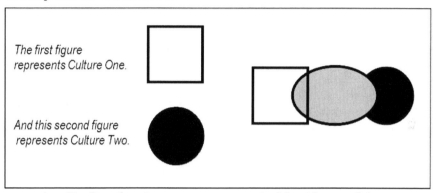

The first figure represents Culture One.

And this second figure represents Culture Two.

opportunity for sharing—as represented by the oval between cultures one and two.

Members from both cultures become involved in common activities—work, recreation, worship, and sharing hospitality. In the growing number of shared experiences, people become involved with each other and a third culture develops. In this setting, ideas can be explained and analyzed. Changes can be made in plans.

When members of that intermediary group return to their original cultures, they'll carry these ideas and plans with them. They become the most effective possible change agents *within their own culture.* They're still members of their own culture group, and so have all the advantages of being an insider in suggesting change. Yet by finding a way to learn from outsiders in the shared third culture, new possibilities are seen for solving group problems.

The key is to create third culture settings that don't destroy a person's participation in his home culture. He must have the opportunity to be involved in new patterns and solutions that he can carry inside his own group. Through the third culture approach he can belong to two groups at the same time. He feels a member of both, participates in both, and is able to learn from both.

These bicultural people are very often the most effective change agents. Many times they're the *only* effective change agents.

Does developing a useful third culture require a massive program? No, a third culture can be built with simple friendship. To build friendship across cultures, the outsider should know how to learn the languages of another culture,[9] develop an ability to learn culture patterns of other people, and make opportunities to share experiences with insiders from that culture.

If interpersonal contacts aren't effective, no large efforts in education, public health, evangelism, agriculture, or anything else will be effective. Success of visible programs depends heavily on the success of non-visible interpersonal relationships. The concept of a third culture can help in building these essential relationships, primarily with simple, interpersonal approaches.

Skill in using another verbal language requires years of study and practice. It may be made somewhat easier, and certainly a more rewarding experience, by recognizing the optimum ways to learn a language. Not only is it best to learn it with the people who use it as their mother tongue (instead of through classrooms and books), but this also gives the delight of sharing in their lives and building shared experiences. Though the language may not be mastered, especially during a short term assignment, the effort of learning is invaluable in achieving the overall goals of cross-cultural ministry.

Learning the cultural patterns of another people must be more than learning about strange foods and unusual customs that astound and amuse the outsider. That's perhaps expected from the tourist, but not from the Christian worker. Developing observational skills is the first step to understanding cultural patterns that are often very different than your own.

"Where do I begin to learn someone else's culture? I'm not an anthropologist!" Almost everyone is aware that cultures are different. That recognition is the place to begin. When you expect things to be different, the differences won't surprise and cause dismay. Those new things should excite you; they're things to be learned, practiced, and perhaps later understood.

When you expect things to be different, you can begin to carefully observe and make note of the things that at first seem so unusual, perhaps even strange. Do make notes! Things that seem unforgettable at first will soon become so familiar that they're overlooked and then forgotten. You need to collect observations, just as some people collect stamps or coins.

From accumulated observations, you'll begin to see patterns of similarities and differences. These will indicate common themes and ideas in the culture. These are building blocks that can give a genuine understanding of the people's ways of living. At least a beginning in the study of cultural anthropology will make this exciting exploration not only easier, but more productive.

You cannot learn another culture by yourself. You'll need help from insiders, people who are part of the culture you're learning. Observing isn't enough; you need to do things with them. Help them with their work whenever possible. Take part in their public feasts and ceremonies. When invited, visit in their homes, and ask them to visit your home.

As you do things with insiders, there will be many good times to ask questions. Understanding will steadily develop as you take part in the insiders' cultural patterns.

This leads to many shared experiences—the fundamental need when building a third culture. These experiences within the insiders' culture are half the material needed to build a third culture. Actually, it's more than half.

More of these shared experiences should be in *their* cultural arena than in yours. Be a change agent who takes the initiative, meeting the insiders in their surroundings rather than expecting them to meet in yours.

Sponsor Needed

Doing these things requires a sponsor, someone within the culture who knows you and is willing to introduce you to his people and their activities. In any setting, he'll inform you of what is happening and guide you in the correct behavior. It's with the sponsor that you'll share most experiences. It's around him or her that a third culture will begin to develop.

A satisfactory sponsor won't be merely anyone available from the insider culture. A sponsor must be firmly part of her own culture, accepted among her own group, and active in their regular activities. At the same time she must speak a second language that you also speak. She must have learned that language outside her own culture, yet remained very much part of her culture.

Be Cautious With "Marginals"

It's tempting to find a sponsor with whom you can communicate very well, but who's not really active in his own people's affairs or completely accepted by her own people. She may have had wide experience outside her group that has pulled her more and more away from her people's way of life. Such a person has become a cultural marginal, participating only superficially in his people's activities and social networks. Rarely is he deeply involved in major debates and decisions. As progressive as such a person appears to the outsider, he's seldom a satisfactory sponsor. She's a bridge that's broken at one end.

Sponsorship demands something in return. Payment appears an easy way to meet your obligations, yet it's very unsatisfactory. Reducing shared experiences to a business transaction eliminates the possibility of real friendship. It largely destroys the basis for a strong third culture.

Help in Return for Help

How do you show thanks when a friend helps you? You look for a way to help him.

In building a third culture, you do exactly the same. When a sponsor shares his home and food, it's good for you to share your home and food with him. He may use several days to help you understand how his people harvest, or build a house, or reach a group decision. In return, introduce him to your family, show him how you grow a garden, or fix a car, or anything else in your "world" in which he shows interest.

Giving and Gaining

It's in sharing your time and telling about yourself that a third culture begins to take firm shape. It's now two-way sharing, rather than you as an outsider intruding into someone's life. You're giving as well as gaining. Friendship is built within an enlarging web of helping each other.

A fruitful missionary to China, Jonathan Goforth, opened his home to visitors and even conducted "tours" to show his home to the Chinese. He explained that some did not consider receiving visitors as real mission work. But he tried hard to make friends with the people—and reaped the results when he went to their villages to preach. Often the people of the village would say, "We were at your place and you showed us through your house, treating us like friends." Then they usually brought him a chair, a table for his Bible, and some tea.

Of course, such friendship cannot be built when one side stays tightly enclosed in its own cultural walls. If contact with the "others" is only a job to do, there's little room for personal relationships to grow. On-the-job time is bought. Social obligation is wiped out by the money given for work done. While that may be the best way to complete a particular task, it's not the way to build a third culture. Strong friendship cannot be bought.

The third culture gives opportunities to plan activities that bring insider and outsider together. Special celebrations or feasts are one possibility. Worshiping together, reading Scripture together, and praying together are other possibilities. Others include viewing films or photographs of common interest, discussing topics, entertaining prominent visitors together, and sports activities. There are many ways to strengthen the third culture group. In these settings, new ideas about development can be informally introduced, and people's needs will be more clearly understood.

Everyone's own culture is comfortable and gives them security. Unless some from each culture show a willingness to move beyond their comfortably secure cultural walls, there can be no third culture. The obligation is on the outside change agent to begin opening ways through the walls. The change agent must start two-way traffic before the insiders will follow. Then a third culture will become a reality, and an effective channel to introduce change is open.

To summarize, here are three straightforward steps:

1. Learn all the languages of a culture.

2. Observe and follow the culture patterns.

3. Find ways to share experiences.

PART THREE

Impossible! Overwhelming!

As we move into another culture—no longer as visitors but now as participants—our personal, internal struggles are likely to become increasingly intense. So much that is expressed or acted is different, even contrary, to the patterns learned from our childhood.

Our challenge now is not only to learn the other culture, but to learn ourselves— and to deal with our inner stress.

Chapter Eight

Culture Shock? Not Me!

It's no joking matter, but culture shock is often the subject of uneasy jokes. It's carelessly used as an explanation for unusual behavior that would be unthinkable "at home." Culture shock, we tell ourselves, is something that happens to other people and isn't very serious. True, it's not usually a life-threatening condition, though at times the stress can lead to critical medical problems.

Normally, stress from culture shock results in excessive tiredness, recurring minor illnesses, erratic behavior, and emotional disturbance. To avoid confusion with medical use of the word *shock*, the problem is correctly referred to here as culture *stress*, instead of the common term "culture shock." Shock is life-threatening; stress, meanwhile, is always present to some degree.

The causes of stress differ as well as its severity. Here, we're dealing with stress caused by unfamiliarity with—and dislike or rejection of—a different culture.

Culture stress is unavoidable and can have serious consequences. If you haven't experienced it, you've had no extended contact with another culture. Perhaps you've kept yourself completely separate from the life of another culture, even when living near it.

Culture stress is normal, not something to be ashamed of or denied. Too many people look upon culture stress as a sign of weakness. They see it as a sign that something's wrong, and so deny having it. Such denial is likely to lead only to more difficulty.

A healthier approach is to simply expect culture stress when you go to a new situation and a new environment. Sometimes it's mild, sometimes very severe. The difference in severity is usually related to the degree of difference between your home culture and the new culture. The less that's known about the new culture, the greater the potential for culture stress.

Some years ago I was asked to go to Hamburg where, as I understood, I was to meet a colleague in Bible translation work. We were to go together to a church agency to discuss the possibilities of funding some research work in which we were both interested. I arrived feeling quite relaxed, looking forward to meeting this friend. But he wasn't there! I looked in every part of the airport, without success. Now what could I do? I understood no German. I didn't know where we were supposed to go. Eventually, I remembered the name of the agency we were to contact—the name was in German.

By now it was late in the afternoon, nearing time for offices to close. I didn't know where in Hamburg the offices were located, nor how to get to wherever that might be. So what could I do now? Where could I sleep tonight? Then perhaps in the morning I could find the church agency offices. I couldn't stay in the airport. I was sure I couldn't find a place to sleep in the city, since I didn't speak German. Quite quickly I found that I intensely disliked Hamburg, its people, its airport, and everything in sight. I decided that Germans were very difficult, and I wanted out of there as quickly as possible. But there was no way out, and I didn't know what to do next.

Finally, I reluctantly went to the information counter for help. To my amazement, the lady on duty spoke good English. I felt considerably more at ease, though I was still very disturbed. She must have realized this as she began to help me find the correct name of the agency that I'd come to visit. She told me which taxi to take, how much I should pay, and carefully told me where I could find a reasonable hotel for the night.

When I finally reached the agency, I found they weren't expecting me and knew nothing about the proposal I brought. At this point culture stress symptoms returned. I thought, "I've heard so much about German efficiency, but where is it? These people seem to understand very little; they're not helpful. And here I am—what now? I've come all this way, and now I don't know what to do."

Eventually, I was introduced to a man who was aware of the project and who knew my friend who was to have met me. Very graciously, he immediately dropped everything he was doing, took me to his home, and showed every possible hospitality. He soon helped me relax. Then we began to talk about the work that had brought me to Hamburg. He was the perfect host and Christian friend.

That whole experience unforgettably demonstrated culture stress. I was disoriented, lacking the ability to understand the cues to guide my behavior correctly in that setting. I couldn't speak the language. I felt that I couldn't even use the telephone because the German way of writing telephone numbers was new to me. I went into the telephone booth but couldn't even manage to dial the number! In that situation, I couldn't even do ordinary, easy things. So I became very resentful of Germans and of Hamburg, and I wanted to leave as quickly as possible.

My experience may sound disturbingly familiar. Sometimes the reaction to culture stress is directed against the place, and at other times against the people. When it's directed against the place, the climate seems intolerable, the scenery dull, the cities dirty and unpleasant. The fascination and delight of seeing what God made in this place is lost, buried under resentment at being there at all.

At other times, culture stress is expressed in dislike of the local people, of their strange or wicked ways, and of their unwillingness to be friendly to you. The good and beautiful among the people isn't recognized, and there's no interest in getting acquainted to find out what to do. The normal reaction is some form of anger with all its damaging results in spirit and body.

In our own culture, we constantly read what is communicated to us through our culture's "signals" or "languages" (which we'll look at more closely later in this book). We've practiced these so well, learning some of them even before we begin to talk, that they're used unconsciously. Greeting others, responding to acquaintances, welcoming friends, accepting an invitation, knowing when a person is joking and when he should be taken seriously—all these signs are read effortlessly. There's little difficulty knowing how to behave in our own culture.

When going to another culture, suddenly the signs are not understood. The familiar signs have different meanings; after a few attempts to act on the meaning known before, we realize we no longer know how to interpret those signs. We sense that we don't know how to behave in this new culture. Those experiences lead directly to culture stress.

At one point during the time we lived in East Africa, we returned to the United States for several months. Our daughter entered high school expecting a good experience— activities, a different approach to teaching, opportunities for music and drama. But we noticed that every day she came from school very tense. We didn't know what was troubling her. One day she explained it: "I just don't know what I'm supposed to do. When the kids stand around and talk, I don't know if I'm supposed to joke or just listen. But I don't understand the jokes. I just don't know what I'm supposed to do." She was experiencing culture stress because of her lack of familiarity with American culture, even though she carried an American passport. She had grown up with Africans and Asians, understanding the signals of those cultures with little difficulty. She only partly understood how to respond to American cultural signals.

It's possible that you may not have experienced much culture stress. If so, it may indicate that you're not really involved with another culture. Whenever you become involved with another culture, culture stress will be present to some degree, and may be very severe.

There's an important reason for taking time to consider culture stress as we learn guides to cross-cultural communication. As principles of better communication are applied, there will be increasing contact with people of other cultures. Culture stress may well become a more severe problem than in the past. If we understand the symptoms, and that this is a normal experience, the problem is much more easily managed. An expected challenge is less dangerous than the wholly unexpected.

Several stages have been identified in becoming involved with another culture. Let's examine these.

Culture Stress: Fascination

First, there's fascination with the other culture. A person thinks, "My, isn't that interesting!" It's a tourist kind of feeling. Everything's fascinating, adventuresome, charming, romantic. You're delighted with your discoveries, the food is good, and you think it's a marvelous way to live. This tourist stage may last, roughly, from two to sixteen weeks.

A "Very Important Person"—a VIP being treated like a VIP—will be with people who speak a language that he also speaks, or translators will be available. He'll be given special treatment and considerable hospitality, and people will be exceptionally courteous. But for the average person who receives ordinary treatment, the tourist stage is quickly left behind. The VIP is told who will interpret his actions to others. The ordinary person is left to himself. Without help, his fascination soon becomes frustration.

Tour groups seem a safe way to visit a new place and to be introduced to a new culture. However, it's so unimaginative to be told, "At 10:35 we'll marvel at the Great Pyramid. Then at 11:00 we'll have opportunity to shop in the exotic shops neighboring the Sphinx," etc.

Why would anyone want to travel that way? Because it avoids culture stress. The group member is told what to do, how to perform. He's insulated. He doesn't become acquainted with anyone locally, so no strange demands are placed on him. At the end of the trip, interesting things are remembered, instead of bewilderment. It's a period of fascination, which is probably the right thing for a tourist.

Christian workers, however, aren't supposed to be tourists. When direct contact is made with another culture, the signs must be read personally. Because the local interpretation of the signals isn't known, very simple things seem complex. Even well-known tasks are performed badly by the newcomer. Frustration and anxiety are the result.

This doesn't last long before the next stage begins— rejection.

Culture Stress: Rejection

Rejection is a dangerous development in culture stress— beware! Unintentionally, you could destroy all that might be accomplished by developing negative and critical attitudes.

Rejection of the culture is expressed in phrases, at first mild but increasingly tinged with bitterness: "These people don't know how to organize." "They don't know how to cook good food; it's surprising anyone here is still alive." "Why can't they do anything right?" The newcomer is quickly convinced of the superiority of his own culture. Contact with the other culture is limited to formal requirements— scheduled meetings, church services, essential business.

Americans visiting Europe as tourists may "reject" European cultures if they stay too long without helpful and sympathetic hosts. International students newly arrived in the United States are often fascinated, delightful guests impressed with the friendliness and hospitality of Americans for the first week or two. As they're left to care for their own needs, confusion and bewilderment grow when they face constant verbal language stress and misunderstanding of almost all other signals—in the classroom, on the streets, and even in the homes of host families. Those who aren't helped through this phase of culture stress reject the host culture, seeking people of their own group "who understand," perhaps developing long-term bitterness and anger toward the host culture.

As they have more direct contact with the host culture, they'll become frustrated and anxious. They don't understand common language idioms, or the habit of slurred speech—gotcha, howyadoin?—or how that last question is asked without waiting for an answer. They don't understand the small differences that can become so confusing: pedestrians passing on the right instead of the left, enthusiasm about football rather than "real" football (soccer), failure to shake hands when meeting or leaving a friend, or the wedding band on the left hand instead of the right. When many of these small differences accumulate, people become confused. The longer they stay the less satisfactory their experience will be. When they return to their home country, they report, "Do you know what they do?"—and then describe everything that confused and bewildered them, confirming how much better their home culture is.

Not understanding the cultural signals that guide acceptable road behavior leads to frustration and anxiety. That leads to rejecting the Italians, or Indians, or Filipinos— at least the driving cultures. On first sight, it seems utter chaos. In Italy, when a visitor asked why the driver ignored the road signs and disobeyed the traffic rules, he was surprised at the question. Then the driver explained some of the things he was watching for. "There's no problem," he insisted. "The other drivers know I wouldn't hit them. If I look at the traffic, they know for sure that I see them. But by not looking, they must give way to me—to protect themselves." He knew the signs. The visitor did not know those signs, so was anxious and even frightened.

So many things in a different country are unfamiliar. How do you bargain for something you want to buy? So many people are constantly asking for rides. Who should ride and who's left behind? Plowing with oxen would be so much better, but the people just don't listen! The list of small and large puzzles becomes longer and longer.

The frequent reaction is to reject the culture. The rejection is expressed by negative judgments about the culture and the people. "This place is disorganized, hopeless. The people can't do anything right. They can't even build a straight wall." Then the newcomer develops the attitude that adaptation is unnecessary. "The problem's theirs, not mine. Why should I take the trouble to learn to act like them? The people here are underdeveloped or we wouldn't be here. They just don't know how to do things correctly." This isn't said openly, but often underlies what is said and done.

The driver of a tractor for an aid organization had a flat tire with no way to repair it, so he walked away and left the tractor. He made no effort to send a message asking for help. He didn't try to radio to the base camp, even though he was less than half a kilometer from the radio. When his supervisor came by several hours later, the driver was resting with some friends in a nearby hut. In Western cultures, reacting to this with impatience and scolding would be understandable, but the visitor in another culture must patiently learn the reasons behind the action. Instead, it's too easy to use the frustrating occasion to condemn all local people as irresponsible. "Here we are, trying to help them, and he doesn't even tell me so we can fix the flat tire! Why can't these people do their job right?"

There seems no reason to learn the local way of thinking or doing things. We think that they should be learning everything from us. This is rejection. We reject what we do not understand. It's a rejection of the culture and of the people, destroying the possibility of being truly helpful.

The rejection phase may last from one to six months. Many people get no further than this in their experience of another culture. This is one of the difficulties with short-term work, whether in a relief program, missions, or a development program. It's also a cause of difficulties in international corporations or government diplomatic services, when personnel are frequently moved.

The policy of quick, short visits without adequate preparation is ill-advised. It prevents personnel from even beginning to truly understand people of other cultures. It may lead to increasing antagonisms because short-term personnel may never pass beyond the rejection phase. Their cross-cultural experience causes them to reject other cultures and glorify their own.

Culture Stress: Regression

Rejection moves to regression with no real break between. In regression, the home environment becomes overwhelmingly important. Personal security is felt only in the home environment, rather than in the local situation. Fears increase, and personal safety becomes a major preoccupation. Some people become afraid of things they would usually ignore—insects, storms, strangers walking by their house, sickness. Almost anything can become a source of fear for a person suffering in the regression phase of culture stress.

In regression, the home place becomes the standard of all that's good and normal; nothing in the local culture is seen as really good. We discover how very excellent everything is in our own culture. We desire things so familiar "at home." For Americans, it's often the intense desire to have a hamburger and a thick milkshake. Social occasions with people of our own culture are urgently needed, and then most conversation is about home and what is happening there. There's more interest in our own culture and its activities than if we were actually home. It has been said, for example, that the British settlers in Kenya and New Zealand were more British than those who stayed in Britain.

Surprisingly, when they do return home, these intense desires soon disappear. The dreams of hamburgers and milkshakes fade, as do all dreams, when we reenter a familiar and comfortable world. The dream is a symptom of rejection; when rejection disappears, there's no longer the need for the dream.

Culture Stress: Hostility

The next stage—hostility—follows quickly. A person becomes resentful of the other culture and inwardly angry. Open criticism follows: "This place is badly organized." Perhaps it's considered "too dictatorial" or "too corrupt."

Anger may be directed against the organization that brought the worker to that location. The group is blamed for all the failings that now are seen so clearly. Development workers become hostile toward their supervisors; missionaries express anger at the mission's "incompetence"; government workers loaned to another government feel their own government has neglected them. The anger is usually not directed at the host culture because it's out of reach. The anger tends to become directed at the leaders of the group who placed the worker in a situation that cannot be understood or controlled.

When culture stress is severe, the worker will begin to focus on the problems of the organization rather than the opportunities for service the organization has opened for him. The administration is suddenly discovered to be inadequate; a clear policy is lacking, there's no sense of direction, their priorities are wrong. The hostility is redirected. The worker is really angry at himself because he can't understand what's going on, and redirects his anger at those who put him in such a bewildering position.

Hostility is directed against fellow workers as well as the organization. Their music, their manners, and their children are annoying. Coworkers don't know their jobs well and are careless about time. Some are thoughtless and leave all the hard work for others. No one else truly understands the situation in the country; others are indifferent to solutions that would help. A chain of small differences causes tensions and even dislikes. The depth of Christian commitment of others in the group is questioned. Those who "think they're so pious and better than everybody else" are resented. The hostile feelings may have been there at home, yet they become more severe when culture stress is involved.

What happens next? This is as far as many people go. They learn to control the hostility so it isn't expressed at embarrassing moments, but the hostility remains. They've learned how to survive to the end of their scheduled term. When it's finished, they go home with a great sigh of relief.

A surprising thing often happens when they reach home. They begin to see things in a different perspective. The challenge of living and working in a difficult place is gone, and they realize the challenge was good. Small faults in people are forgotten and warm friendships are remembered. After two or three months, a new contract may be signed, and return to cross-cultural living is eagerly anticipated.

Is it necessary, then, to go home before hostility can be overcome? No one is effective as a missionary or development worker while carrying a load of hostility and anger. Sermons may be preached, roads may be built, wells dug, and buildings constructed, but the real issues of development are with people's attitudes. If the worker's attitude is wrong, how is a right attitude created in other people?

CULTURE STRESS	WEEKS	
EXPLORATORY	0-8	Anticipation
		Fascination
		Bewilderment
CRISIS	9-16	Rejection
	17-24	Regression
	20-28	Hostility
ADJUSTMENT	16+	Learning
BICULTURAL	20 +	Involvement

Chapter Nine

Curing the Invisible Illness

Culture stress can cause physical illness and psychological disturbances. In extreme cases, it can cause severe mental illness. It's not a thing to be ignored, nor a thing to be ashamed of. It's the result of stress, so the causes of that stress must be reduced or eliminated.

An effective way to overcome culture stress is learning to correctly read the signals of another culture. (These twelve "signal systems" are introduced and discussed in Chapters 10 and 11.) The person who determines to be a learner of the culture's signal systems from the very beginning will largely escape severe symptoms of culture stress.

Learning can help overcome hostility. As the clues to guide behavior are understood, bewilderment lessens and hostility turns to tolerance. It's easier to recognize that people are merely different, not worse or better. They're not utterly ignorant Indonesians, loud Americans, or silent Swedes. The differences may even be appreciated! This is often the first healthy sign in recovery from culture stress. The home culture is still thought to be best—but some good things are seen in the new culture.

Group Help for Prevention and Recovery

What practical help can coworkers give in overcoming the problem of cultural stress?

The simple cure requires some self-discipline as well as the encouragement of coworkers. Develop the self-discipline to become a learner. Among the people where you're working, observe the use of the twelve signal systems that you'll see described in chapters 10 and 11. Share those signals and meanings learned. Take time to discuss with coworkers what has been learned. Ask those of the other culture about things that were confusing or puzzling. Though culture stress frequently leads to misunderstandings, a willingness to ask for help demonstrates the readiness to learn and increases trust in your motives.

Developing willingness to share questions and ask about confusing behaviors can also help in reducing tensions between coworkers that directly or indirectly developed because of culture stress. Go over your notes together and share insights into the behavior of the local people, and how they use the signal systems. Not only will you be able to communicate more effectively, you'll also reduce problems among yourselves.

Small learning groups can include a sharing of problem solutions. Or perhaps, if the problem hasn't been solved, discussion with others may show the way through the difficulty. In these ways, interpersonal support networks are built among the workers. These should not be large groups— just four to twelve people who build friendship and trust as they together learn the best ways to function in another culture.

The next stage should be adjustment. Adjustment cannot occur, of course, until you begin to learn the other culture. As long as you continue to learn, there will be continuing adjustment increasing your comfort within another culture.

Living in Two Cultures

How long does it take to be able to live in two cultures? A person cannot, and should not, forget his own culture.

Within six to twelve months, enough of the other culture can be learned to operate comfortably there, though there's still much to learn in reaching the core (heart) of the culture.

Healthy adjustment doesn't mean leaving the home culture behind, abandoning your own culture. It's a matter of learning to operate in two cultures. The successful cross-cultural worker becomes a bicultural individual. Stress gradually decreases, and with continued learning and adjustment, hostility decreases. The well-adjusted person discovers that he's reluctant to leave even when the term of service is completed.

Can Adjustment Be *Too* Complete?

When much is learned about the people, there's growing relief. It's possible to operate in another culture with comfort! Constant frustration and anxiety disappear. Have all the problems of culture stress now ended? No, not quite.

Enthusiastic use of new cultural knowledge may lead to over-compensation for still being a foreigner. So the "reluctant foreigner" begins to reject his own culture, in part or all. Emotionally and psychologically, that reaction may be equally as dangerous as the initial rejection of the other culture.

This response to culture stress has been observed among students studying in a foreign culture. During the first months they're fascinated with their experience; then they move into a period of rejection. If they stay for a longer period, perhaps two years or more, they learn the new culture so well that they begin to think of it as their own culture. The students reject their home culture, losing much of their ability to operate easily in their home environment. When they do go home, time must be allowed for what has been called "reverse culture stress." The same experience is frequent among missionaries and sometimes development workers.

Are Some People Affected More than Others?

One finding of research into cultural adjustment is that the ability to accept uncertainty is directly related to the ability to live successfully in another culture. People who cannot accept uncertainty will rarely be successful cross-cultural workers, since the ability to live with uncertainty is necessary for cultural adaptation. Not knowing what's happening at all times is disturbing for some people, yet not as difficult for others. This psychological difference between individuals is a factor in susceptibility to culture stress.

Research has also found that self-image is related to the effects of culture stress. The person with a good self-image—the ability to view oneself realistically and favorably—is less likely to suffer from culture stress. In entering another culture, there's little to support a favorable view of yourself. You cannot talk clearly, you don't understand subtle signals between people, and laughter seems directed at you since you certainly cannot understand the jokes that are shared. Those who think well of themselves only when others approve of them will have an especially difficult time with culture stress. In a new culture, it's difficult to know if you're accepted and approved, or the object of laughter and perhaps scorn.

The work we're doing also affects the degree to which culture stress affects us. An administrator in a large organization probably has less culture stress than a village medical worker. The administrator is often treated as a VIP, receiving hospitality instead of non-cooperation or hostility. Part of hospitality is to ease the misunderstandings that normally occur. Many villagers have so little experience of other cultures that they usually don't know how to ease an outsider's difficulties. Thus the worker who's in closer contact with another culture will probably experience greater culture stress.

Husbands usually have less culture stress than wives. The difference is not between men and women, but between the roles played by each. Husbands usually have less culture stress because they have professional duties that provide emotional security as they contact another culture. A builder knows he's going to build; a doctor knows he's going to deal with sickness. The wife, on the other hand, is still in the home, whether it's in Hiliu, Oslo, or Singapore. In the new place she doesn't know how to operate her household, how to buy food months in advance, how to rid the kitchen of cockroaches, and countless other unknowns. She has fewer familiar routines than does her husband. Because she has less contact with the local culture, she may have a harder time in adjustment. There is reason to expect that husbands would have the same challenges if roles are reversed.

Culture Stress: Not for You Alone

Culture stress doesn't happen only to foreign workers; it also happens to nationals working with the foreigners. Even though it's their homeland and home culture, they're working largely in the foreign workers' program and thus his culture. As a result, this may create considerable culture stress. The foreigners' ways seem strange. The way they speak and give directions, all the things that are natural to the foreigners in working with one another, are confusing to the national. It is important to recognize that the problem of culture stress applies to the national working with foreigners, as well as to the foreigner in a new land and culture. It's necessary to be aware of those difficulties as well as those of your family and colleagues.

I've heard it said by Africans, "So and so is a good missionary, we can understand him." I'd always thought of it in terms of the missionary understanding the Africans. With fuller experience of African life, it became clear that the ability to understand the missionary was equally important. Even the unusual person who never experiences culture stress must recognize that national colleagues will suffer some culture stress from working with the foreigner. Give the help you would want for yourself.

PART FOUR

Beginning to Learn

Knowledge, understanding, and wisdom are triplets that should never be separated. Each is a critical part of introducing change to another culture; each is a gift from God—when we're ready to receive them. "For the LORD gives wisdom, and from his mouth come knowledge and understanding" (Proverbs 2:6). Without those gifts, any form of development ministry will be temporary at best.

How can we prepare to gain understanding?

First, we need to gain at least some knowledge. Then we can develop understanding, to use knowledge meaningfully. Wisdom develops as we walk with the people and with God. Note His promise: "Then you will understand what is right and just and fair—every good path. For wisdom will enter your heart, and knowledge will be pleasant to your soul. Discretion will protect you, and understanding will guard you. Wisdom will save you from the ways of wicked men, from men whose words are perverse"(2:9-12).

These "triplets" are essential; how do I welcome them? By involvement with people and with God. Sharp, analytical tools of knowledge help us toward effective communication with other cultures. The next four chapters briefly outline two such tools.

First, the "twelve signal systems"—the twelve languages of culture—are the beginning tools for discerning the underlying behaviors and beliefs of a culture.

Second, the "cultural onion" is a model of culture to guide you in learning the invisible, controlling environment that seems to blanket everything like a fog. We see shapes without knowing what they really are. But with this map we can begin to know.

Chapter Ten

Twelve Languages of Culture

What are the different ways by which people transfer information? Speech and pictures, writing, drama, audio and video recordings, textbooks—the list of possible ways to share information seems almost endless.

All these methods are included in twelve different systems of signals within which nearly all human communication occurs. These twelve signal systems, or languages of culture, can be listed simply, but a lifetime can be spent mastering the use of possible combinations of these languages of culture.

Here are the twelve:

Verbal—speech, use of the spoken word.

Written—words preserved with a script, the written word.

Numeric—use of numbers to convey meaning.

Pictorial—drawings and pictures.

Audio—sounds and music.

Artifactual—the use of objects.

Kinesic—body motion in all its varieties.

Optical—use of color and light.

Tactile—touch and the sense of feel.

Spatial—use of space to give information.

Temporal—using time to give a message

Olfactory—using taste and smell.

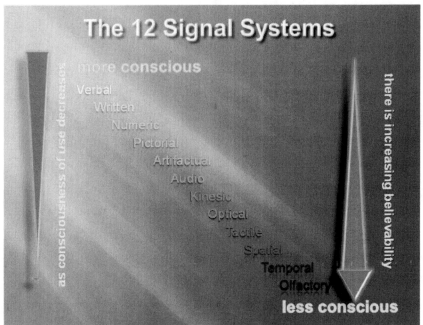

The 12 Signal Systems

more conscious

as consciousness of use decreases

Verbal
Written
Numeric
Pictorial
Artifactual
Audio
Kinesic
Optical
Tactile
Spatial
Temporal
Olfactory

there is increasing believability

less conscious

Knowing these signals or languages is a good beginning, but the ability to recognize them in every culture is what gives this tool practical value. Each "signal" or "language" differs from culture to culture in the way it's used and the form in which it's expressed. Even when a particular signal appears to be the same or similar in different cultures, it probably has a significantly different meaning. Thus, learning these language is of little value if the meaning and common usage are not also learned.

The Verbal System

Verbal is human speech, the most efficient system of interpersonal communication. Today, mankind uses between 3,000 and 5,000 different languages, the exact number depending on the classification system used. Every language has its own strength and beauty of expression related to the experience and values of the people speaking it.

The Written System

Writing is simply the use of special symbols to represent human speech. Many different systems have been used for writing, with perhaps fifty currently in use around the world. In addition, there are many ancient scripts no longer in daily use, such as cuneiform, hieroglyphics, and runic. Orthography is a formal study centering on written systems of communication.

It has been said that in Africa no form of writing has emerged. That's not correct. One form, Amharic of Ethiopia, received some influence from Arabia, across the Red Sea. And at least four other forms of written language developed in Africa. One is a system of pictographic symbols or signs formerly used widely across Bantu Africa. Many of these symbols are still used in designs, even where people have lost the original significance of the symbol.

Until the introduction of the Roman alphabet, these were used by some leaders to send and receive messages. Among Zulus the patterns were worked in beads. It's said that young women sent these as messages of love to their beloved. The famous designs on the wall of the Zimbabwe ruins are in fact designs that indicate the idea of eternity, or the river of life. This form of writing is now mostly neglected; the Roman alphabet is more efficient and flexible.

A system of symbols developed on Africa's West Coast, in the nation of Ghana, is still utilized on public buildings, in jewelry, and elsewhere. The symbol here for God's omnipotence and power is an example.

The Numeric System

Numbers and number systems are a deliberate way of communicating. Mathematics is the formal study of the numeric system, using numbers to express ideas through relationships and values. The numeric system permits very precise description, both of intangible ideas and tangible things. Numbers can also be used individually to express and send a message. This is the foundation of digital systems that are bringing major changes to the mechanics of communication.

Certain numbers have distinctive meanings. The number three in Western cultures often speaks of the Trinity. In some places, three quick sounds are used as a danger signal or warning (as in the Morse Code's familiar "SOS" pattern of sounds: three short, three long, three short). Seven is the biblical number of perfection, of completion. And 666 is the mark of the beast, the anti-Christ. The Cabalists of the Middle Ages carried numerology to an extreme, interpreting Scriptures by the numeric patterns of its words. Numbers were used as the key to prophecy and hidden secrets of the world.

Different numbers have special significance among different cultures. For example, among Sudan's Lotuho, the number four indicates completion in ritual ceremonies. If the wrong number of things is grouped together, it's considered to bring misfortune.

The Pictorial System

An artist may reflect his environment, but more significantly, the artist shows his cultural perception of the environment. Chinese art is very different from African; African art is different from European, even when the same subject or scene is portrayed.

We tend to assume that pictures are universal; they are not. Pictures don't have the same meaning for all people. Even the same picture will communicate different things to different people.

Illustrations were prepared by the United Bible Societies to depict Luke 15, the "lost things" chapter, for use in Central Africa. In the picture of the lost son, the father was shown rushing forward, extending his arms to embrace the son.

This picture was shown to seventy Central Africans of all ages, giving no explanation of the purpose of the picture. When asked what was happening in the picture, the most common explanation was, "Well, the father is very angry with his son and is coming to crush him." There was no thought of embracing.

Another artist was asked to draw the same scene, this time within an African cultural understanding. In that picture, the son kneels before the father. The father receives him, placing his hand on the son's shoulder. When this picture was shown, people immediately understood the story being told.

Viewers can easily misunderstand the meaning of a picture. There's no such thing as a universal pictorial alphabet. Each culture will express ideas in its own pictorial idiom.

Many times in African art the human figure will be greatly elongated. In carvings, the head or another part of the body is frequently enlarged in relation to the rest of the figure. Such art is sometimes dismissed as "primitive." This reaction totally misses the significance of the design. The human figure is frequently made unusually tall in African art to show the dominance of the human over other aspects of creation. This reflects the idea that the human is intended to have dominion over his world. Even mass-produced tourist carvings have African ideas behind them that sometimes appear grotesque to Western eyes.

Haida and the art of Canada's First Nations can be better understood by remembering that the artist tries to show the essence of the subject, rather than what it looks like to the eye. Thus a carving may show the spirit of a clan, emphasizing the aspects of the clan considered important. It's the spirit of the clan's totem animal that's expressed in the graceful, often geometric portrayals.

Indian art on the other hand concentrates on patterns. Chinese art typically expresses philosophical ideas, using symbols understood in Chinese culture.

Each cultural group has similar emphases in its art forms. To use pictorial communication effectively, these differing forms need to be understood.

The Audio System

Audio communication includes not only music, but also various individual signals such as whistles and bells.

Music is a powerful way not only to give information, but especially to build emotion. "Music affects us on every level: neurological, physiological, aesthetic, and emotional."[10] "Researchers have now proved that listening to your favorite melodies can trigger the brain to release large amounts of dopamine, a chemical that sends 'feel good' signals to the rest of the body and plays a role in both motivation and addiction."[11]

The same music doesn't affect all of us in the same way. Our response to music depends on personal experience and the culture or cultures in which we live. Drums are one example. They can be used to maintain a steady rhythm or to stir excitement. They can also be used very precisely to send messages. How drums are used, and how they're heard, depends on the setting and culture where they're played.

Both the rhythm and the tone of drums are good examples of audio communication. Among peoples of the Sahel regions of Africa, particular drum rhythms can be played only by certain clans at special times. In Lotuho villages, for example, each section of the village has its own rhythm to be played on its own set of drums. These sets normally have six drums, which are kept in the *ahadufa* (drum house). They're referred to as one father, five children. If a person from another section of the village plays that rhythm, he'll be severely punished. It's a cause for quarreling and fighting.

Music, of course, is a formalized system of audio communication used by all peoples. Flute, whistles, clapping, the trills of the women—all are music forms used as communication.

The tone of voice is also part of audio communication. If a friend says, "What do *you* think of that?" one meaning is given. But if he says, "What do you think of *that?*" a different meaning is given.

The Artifactual System

In the artifactual system, objects are used to communicate a message. Look at a friend for a moment. Can you tell anything just by looking at the objects around him? His clothing tells us something about personal tastes and his work. His books, pens, papers—all these things are artifactual communication.

At a Coptic service in Trinity Cathedral in Addis Ababa, a large number of artifacts were seen during worship. The cross was used, along with a bell, the Bible, candles, tapers, incense, to name a very few. There were three elements in the communion. In addition to the widely used bread and wine, water was also used, as participants ceremonially washed their hands as preparation for communion. Each object represented a teaching of the Coptic Church and served as a reminder of that teaching.

Artifacts don't communicate the same way in different cultures. The same object may mean different things. Americans wear the wedding ring on the third finger of the left hand; Norwegians wear the wedding ring on the right hand. Does that indicate that Norwegians use the ring only for decoration? Of course not. Such a small difference, but it's the kind of difference that can lead to misunderstanding.

The furniture in a home, the objects around the home, the way it's decorated—all these things indicate a great deal about the people living there. Even the kind of transport used speaks much about the person. In fact, market researchers in Western countries have found that the kind of home, the kind of job, and many of the interests of a person can be predicted by observing the type of car he drives.

A particular wood sculpture created by a Kenyan artist appeared to be an impossibly grotesque human figure. It was elongated, with a head where the head should be plus another head in the stomach area, which was fat. Each of the very wide mouths had great teeth sticking out. A knowledgeable African man carefully explained the figure: It represented a greedy human, thus the huge mouth in the fat stomach. The teeth were grabbing everything for itself. The carving was a condemnation of human greed, he explained, and not at all grotesque or primitive. In fact, it accurately and emotionally expressed African ideas about oppressive leaders.

The Kinesic System

Kinesics is a technical word for the use of body motion to communicate. Dance is a form of kinesics. Dance as a communicative mode has been most highly developed in East Asian countries such as India, Thailand, and Indonesia. There the stories of their religions are conveyed by dance-actors with carefully controlled motions and postures. Ballet, as developed in Western countries, is another form of kinesic communication. Less structured and less predictable dance forms often express enthusiasm, happiness, and other emotions in Western cultures.

In addition, much kinesic communication is far simpler than these structured and more formal usages. The posture of a person's body tells much about the person's health, present attitude, and whether he likes or dislikes the person to whom he's speaking. Teachers and preachers soon learn that they should watch the kinesics of their audience. By noticing posture, placement of hands, and other body movements, the experienced speaker receives a good indication of audience interest.

A Swedish friend said that he could always tell Americans by the way they walk. "You all walk as if you're going to a shoot-out," he laughed; "your hand is ready to jerk down and pull out your revolver!"

It's often true that culture and nationality are revealed by body posture and movement. A special dance of Zulu young men is fascinating—there's a great deal of motion, yet the men move slowly. Many parts of their body are involved, yet their feet take only small steps.

Signals given with different parts of the body mean many different things. Hands, feet, chin, head, shoulder—all can be moved in a way that conveys specific information. For example, how tall are your children? "About that tall," we'll say, usually indicated with an extended hand, palm down. But in some cultures, that kind of signal indicates that you don't want them to grow up. That kinesic signal is interpreted as putting a curse upon them—that you don't want them to grow taller. In that culture, the parents instead will hold out their hand with the fingers pointed upward, the tip of the fingers indicating the height of their children. These "small" differences in use of kinesics can make a big difference in understanding.

Pointing directly with the index finger at a person is not merely rude in many parts of Africa, but considered a threatening gesture. In general, it's safer to point with the chin or indicate in some other way the direction or object to which you are referring.

Kinesics are of such great importance in communicating that it's wise to carefully observe how kinesics are used by the people among whom you're living. Make notes of what you see, and compare your notes with those of fellow workers to aid in more quickly improving communication.

Chapter Eleven

More Languages of Culture

As we've stated, the real building blocks of communication are twelve signal systems or languages of cultures, rather than the kinds of tools with which we're so often preoccupied. Projectors, microphones, amplifiers, computers, printers, copy machines—these are useful devices, yet they can only extend the reach of the signals that actually carry the message. With such devices, more people can receive the signals in more places, but extending the message will be meaningless if the basic twelve signal systems (languages of culture) aren't adequately used in the original design of the message.

In Chapter 10, seven of those twelve signals were introduced. The remaining five are less obviously carriers of information. They do, however, commonly carry much of the emotional content of communication.

The Optical System

Light and color communicate meaning, often with strong psychological power. The particular meaning assigned to a color varies from one culture to another. Zulus, for example, do not normally prefer green. To them, green is a neutral color with no real strength or content. It's not considered attractive. Red would be chosen instead, to express vigor and force.

People who broke away from the Zulus about 170 years ago do not like to use red. To them, red represents blood, disturbance, and turmoil. They would rather use green and blue shades for decoration and clothing.

Among the Yoruba people of Nigeria, green and blue are not only liked, they are the royal colors. Meanwhile the Swazi consider reddish-orange to be the royal colors, whereas in Europe, purple represents royalty.

Not only is the use of color different in different cultures, but the psychological impact of color differs. Blue isn't always considered a restful color—that's a European concept. Red likewise isn't always an exciting, turbulent color; the Chinese consider it the color of good fortune. Black represents mourning and sadness in the West; in the East, white is used for the same purpose.

The Tactile System

Touch is a language with the ability to carry a highly emotional message. It would be difficult to learn mathematics by touch, or geography, or any subject that required a high "load" of information to successfully transfer a factual message. Still, those who are blind must do exactly that. The use of touch in reading Braille writing utilizes the Tactile System. The sense of touch in the fingers reads information efficiently. Such capability, however, is incidental to Touch's primary role to carry an emotional message.

We communicate by touch. With our loved ones we hold hands, kiss, and hug. A child may be spanked as a form of discipline. In anger, blows may be exchanged. At other times, we protect ourselves from being touched because we don't like the person or persons attempting to touch us. We communicate our desire to be alone by not letting anyone touch us, considering it an invasion of our privacy.

Americans occasionally shake hands, but Europeans shake hands at every opportunity—or so it seems to Americans. Good male friends in Africa often hold hands while walking together. To do so in European cultures is objectionable, indicating homosexuality. A man and woman do not touch each other in public throughout most of Africa even if they're husband and wife. Yet in some Western countries, men will put their arm around their wife in public, even in church!

The Spatial System

What's the right distance between two people for a friendly conversation?

In Northern Europe, friends would stand three to four feet apart. For Americans, the distance is about two and one-half to three feet apart. But in Latin Countries, friends stand about eighteen inches apart while conversing.

What happens when people of different cultures talk together, if they don't understand this differing use of space? The story has often been told of a diplomatic reception attended by people of various nationalities. A Latin American approached a German to talk in a friendly fashion, but the German unconsciously stepped backward for a more comfortable sense of space. Then the Latin American stepped further forward to maintain the right friendly distance. Again, the German backed up. So it went, until eventually the German had been walked around the room backwards!

While this was going on, an attitude developed in the Latin's subconscious: "Why is he unfriendly? Why is he so distant from me?" The German on the other hand felt that the Latin was too pushy and dominant, trying too hard to force acceptance of his ideas. Both had an unrecognized reaction of discomfort that could have easily become dislike—all because of differing use of the spatial signal system.

We all maintain a certain personal space surrounding us. The size of it varies depending on our culture and the circumstances of a particular moment. It's necessary to remember this space if we're to avoid unconsciously offending another person by invading "their" space. Since the size of this space varies in different cultures, it's vital to learn what the dimensions of personal space are in the culture where you're learning to work and live.

The spatial signal system is also seen in many other areas of culture. The size of offices and their location in a building—at the top floor or on the ground, and on an outside corner with lots of windows or somewhere more recessed—is a strong carrier of information in Western cultures. In English we even use the idiom "the man at the top" to refer to the head of an organization—a reference to spatial communication.

Walking into a business office, you may find a helpful man sitting behind a small desk piled high with work. You may respond, "Thank you very much for your assistance, but I want to talk to the person in charge." You're seeking someone at the big desk in the big room, because that person (presumably) is the one with influence. The spatial signals from the first man do not speak of decision-making power—small desk, visible clutter of work, easy accessibility to the public.

Towns and cities are planned differently in different cultures. Even with the same amount of land and the same conditions of land and climate, each cultural group will build quite differently. Italians frequently build high apartment buildings—four, five, and six floors—even in small towns where there are many miles of relatively empty countryside around the village. This reflects their cultural desire to live close together. On the other hand, family housing in small towns of Germany is more often in individual houses separate from their neighbors.

In America, each family usually prefers to live independently, on their own piece of ground. American cities spread far into the countryside, and small towns lack the high buildings seen in Italy.

The Lotuho live in villages built fairly densely, with houses close together. The Xhosa people of Southern Africa spread their homes across the countryside, with a much wider distance between neighbors.

The Temporal System

Time surely must be the same everywhere in the world. After all, it's based on movement of the sun and stars, and accurately measured, whether displayed on round dials, liquid crystal displays, great tower clocks, or in works of art wrought in precious stones and metals. Time is a precious thing, and our artifactual way of displaying it underlines how much we value it.

Time may be the same everywhere, but it isn't *used* the same way everywhere. The differing ways of using time are an important system of signals in communication. As it did for the rabbit of *Alice In Wonderland*, our view of time indicates much about us.

European cultures have many words for time and its units—hours, minutes, seconds, milliseconds, etc. Many cultures of Asia and Africa have not, in the past, had words for such divisions. Recognized time units were much larger—before dawn, early dawn, morning, and so on. Time was fixed by the position of the sun, a measurement that could only be approximate. To set a meeting time, people pointed to "there"—indicating where the sun would be in the sky when they met. There was little need for more accurate fixing of time. That, of course, has changed in recent decades to accommodate the widespread technologies that demand more accurate time measurement.

It's not only the difference between accuracy of measuring time that makes for cultural differences in use of time. The Swiss and Germans have long been known for their great punctuality; being late by more than five minutes for an appointment is considered quite discourteous. The English and Americans have the same kind of watches as the Swiss and Germans, though they prefer not to be so exact in their daily use of time. Five minutes late for most appointments scarcely calls for an apology. The peoples of southern Africa have considered it impolite to come to a public meeting at exactly the hour it was announced to begin. Fifteen to thirty minutes late was often acceptable.

The confusion that occurs when different cultures meet is understandable; when an appointment or meeting is scheduled, a good question to ask is, "Whose time are we following?"

The Olfactory System

Taste and smell are powerful ways to carry emotionally laden information. In most of Asia and Africa, if you never drink coffee or tea with people, or never share their food, it sends a strong message that you don't wish to have personal contact. Friendly relationships can be built by giving others something to drink, and inviting them to your table for a meal.

The kind of food served also carries a message. Roasting goat meat over a fire and serving it with bread or a local bread substitute is enjoyed both for the food and for the friendliness it signals. In America, if you serve a nicely made casserole of macaroni and cheese, some will politely eat but perhaps comment to friends afterward, "They didn't give me real food." On the other hand, serving fancy foods won't impress people with your friendliness nearly as much as serving something familiar and appreciated.

Beef, by the way, is reserved for weddings or funerals in many parts of Africa. To serve beef is like giving away the money in your bank account to your guests. You shouldn't eat your wealth. Goats, however, aren't considered wealth in the same way as cattle.

Smell is closely related to food and taste, including things used exclusively to create pleasant feelings, such as perfume. In Western cultures, women use perfume, but usually not men. Men use aftershave lotion! Some scents are appropriate for women and not for men. Men consider it manly to smell like a pine tree or a leather saddle; women are considered to be more feminine if they use scents such as violet, rose, and gardenia.

The appropriateness of a scent is culturally related. In India, men prefer to use the scents of rose or coconut. Those are considered manly, though in the West a man using those scents would be thought effeminate.

Principles in Using the Signal Systems

Understanding the following principles will give further insight into the twelve signal systems, the languages of culture.

1. We rarely use a single signal system by itself. In normal interpersonal communication, we use two or more of these systems at the same time.

One language reinforces another, or carries information that cannot be carried by other systems. The total message is the result of the combination of signals. In teaching a class, for example, the teacher uses verbal, kinesic, written, and probably artifactual, pictorial, optical, spatial, and temporal systems. On some occasions, the teacher may also use numeric, audio, tactile, and perhaps olfactory. Each of the systems complements and supports the others.

2. When two, three, or several signal systems are used at the same time, the systems may contradict each other.

This occurs when the systems don't complement and support each other. Instead, the signals from one system may directly contradict the signals from another system. This kind of contradiction between signal systems is the cause of many misunderstandings in interpersonal communication, especially between people from different cultures.

Verbal and audio systems frequently contradict each other: *"Really?* Did you find *that* interesting? How *nice* that you enjoyed it!" What was communicated? The words said, "I think it's great that you liked it." But the audio system, the tone of the voice in this case, indicated, "That's a silly thing to like!"

3. When signal systems contradict each other, we tend to believe the less consciously used signal system. If while using the verbal system, for example, kinesic signals contradict the verbal, we'll normally believe the kinesic.

These twelve signal systems have been listed in this book in order of decreasing consciousness of use. For example, the verbal is almost always consciously used, while the olfactory is seldom consciously used as deliberate communication. The written system is more consciously used than the kinesic, tactile, or spatial.

Perhaps someone comments, "Mr. X is a person I don't really trust. Don't always believe what he says; you can't be sure he really means it." What does this mean, in light of the signal systems? Simply that Mr. X's verbal system is repeatedly contradicted by the less consciously used kinesic, spatial, or tactile signals.

This often occurs in cross-cultural communication. A person may genuinely mean what he says verbally, but listeners interpret his audio, kinesic, temporal, tactile, and spatial messages in a different way than he believes possible. As a result, they don't believe what he's saying. This is a cause for many accusations of insincerity about "other people." "You can't trust them"—those words are said by every group about other groups because we don't know how to correctly read the other group's signals.

Consider what may be understood in many nations by the signals sent from groups involved in missions or relief or development. "We care about you; that's why we're here to build roads, dig wells, build schools, and improve your crops. We want to help care for your sicknesses, and show you the love of Christ in every way we can." It has often been pointed out that what we do speaks so loudly that others cannot hear what we say. These efforts in development are intended to speak of how Christ loves all men.

However, in the use of kinesic, spatial, tactile, olfactory, and all the other systems, is our intended message unknowingly contradicted? It's possible that the people may understand some signals to say, "We don't want to be too close to you, or too involved. We don't really trust you." Which signals will be believed? The less consciously used systems, not the more consciously used verbal system. The good that's being attempted may be lost because of misunderstanding of signal systems.

4. All signal systems carry both rational and emotional information, though in unequal amounts.

In all cultures, there are two kinds of responses to the information carried—a rational response and an emotional response. Some signal systems are more likely to stimulate an emotional response, others a rational response. The written is normally heavy with information at the rational level. But an emotional response may be also present, as in cultures where the message will be believed because it is written. In other cultures, it will be *dis*believed precisely because it's written, which is an equally emotional response.

The spatial, temporal, and olfactory systems are heavily emotional in most cultures. Misuse of space can cause a person's temper to rise, without the person knowing why he's angry. There's a strong emotional reaction with little or no understanding of what's happening.

The spoken word can be used not only to describe emotion, but also to convey emotion. When combined with audio, the verbal system carries a remarkable amount of emotional as well as rational content.

Both emotion and reason are necessary in effective communication. The twelve signal systems carry both kinds of information, though the proportion of each varies from situation to situation and culture to culture. It is important to note that cultures functioning within contextual logic (see Chapter 5) are often more aware of all of the signal systems being used than the cultures, primarily Western, that stress linear logic. The contextual cultures integrate much more readily all the dimensions of communication apparent in the twelve signal systems. That "total view" is essential to contextual logic.

William Barclay expresses well the importance of both aspects of the languages of culture: "Even when a man cannot understand with his intellect, he can still feel with his heart. It is better to love Jesus than to love theories about Him."[12]

We're attempting to communicate clearly an infinite message to finite men, the message of Jesus Christ. We must communicate that message in many different cultures and subcultures, to tens of thousands of individuals each with a different way of seeing the world. The very least we can do is to understand how communication occurs, to understand the raw materials of communication with which we must work.

This is why these twelve signal systems have been identified. Understanding these broad principles can free us from fruitless imitation of what's done elsewhere. We can be free to create the best combination of signals to communicate the love of God in Jesus Christ for each cultural situation.

Chapter Twelve

The Cultural Onion

So much to understand! We encounter such a jumble of impressions and experiences: friendship, but also disloyalty, dislike, and even hatred; floods as well as drought; the quiet beauty of fields and trees and fruit, along with the raging of rivers and the dangers of deserts and rocky heights. Fighting and threats, as well as help and comfort. The world seems a mass of buzzing, threatening, peaceful, distracting confusion.

If we fully saw, heard, felt, smelled, or touched all of this— if we functionally *and* structurally perceived everything—we would be driven "out of our minds." We simply couldn't mentally process so many stimuli. We must select, never structurally perceiving some things, choosing to ignore other things, and deciding to forget still others. We can select only a few for our attention and response.

Some things come to us again and again. We must respond as easily as possible to those, almost automatically. Our energy and time cannot be used to make a new decision each time the same thing happens. A pattern emerges, and that pattern provides a way to respond with little thought.

We're hungry in the morning. It's foolish in normal living to stop, consider, and decide what to do about that hunger— it's a familiar situation. So we simply eat or drink, and call it breakfast. Day after day, that pattern handles our stimulus of hunger in the morning.

In some societies, no food or drink is taken until the middle of the morning, after three or four hours of work. That's another pattern for handling the same stimulus of hunger. Either way, the decision is not whether to eat, but only when and what to eat. Even what to eat is seldom considered—often because there's no choice, and at other places and times because the familiar is more satisfying. Patterns become habits that simplify living.

Culture is a synthesis of many habits and patterns, all necessary to handle the impossible complexity of life. It helps us make necessary decisions for survival and even comfort, without expending our time and energy on repeated problems.

And thus, culture is a pattern for survival. It's a pattern for preserving and improving one's life and for maintaining relationships with other people. It provides a pattern for relating to our total environment. Culture is far more than interesting customs that differ from place to place. Without culture, humans would not survive.

Culture is learned behavior. When we're young, we watch how others handle a situation, then we try to do the same. We learn their attitudes toward all that's around them, and those attitudes gradually become ours as we mature. We learn the ability to interact with the world that surrounds us.

There are usually many different possibilities for responding to common problems and opportunities. But alternatives aren't considered when cultural patterns are already established. We simply respond according to patterns already learned in our culture. Modified very slowly, patterns will continue as long as they continue satisfying people's needs. Of course, if the pattern doesn't bring satisfaction and needs aren't met, people seek a different way. Culture change is most rapid at the times when old patterns no longer meet current needs.

Especially when people move from rural areas to crowded urban areas, traditional ways no longer meet needs. People from multiple ethnic backgrounds, often with different home languages, are intermingled. Living skills essential in rural areas are no longer useful, and previously unimagined abilities must be developed.

Rapid change is essential to survival. As old patterns are scorned and discarded, new patterns are attempted— sometimes with positive results, but often with poor outcomes.

Even when culture is changing, only limited possibilities for change are recognized. Each culture is able to perceive only certain things. Another culture in the same situation sees different possibilities. Culture change happens only within the possibilities recognized by the culture itself, not by someone from outside that culture.

In common with many other cultures, the Lotuho of South Sudan are constantly faced with the possibility of drought and famine because of erratic rainfall patterns. So the *hobu ahide* (rainmaker) has a prominent place in their lives. Rain means life and survival. Anything that would threaten regular rainfall must be avoided. The Lotuho seek to live so that the *hobu ahide* and the God who sends rain will not be offended.

Norwegian aid workers in the same area near the Nile also recognize the importance of rain. But they don't select a rainmaker and don't believe their social behavior will affect the rainfall. Instead they bring equipment to drill holes in the earth—hoping to find water beneath the surface instead of from the sky!

Meanwhile, to the north, the Arabic peoples in Sudan suggest that water could be pumped out of the Nile's year-round flow, or that ditches could divert part of the river's water to the gardens and fields where food crops are grown.

A rainmaker, digging of wells, and diversion of existing water flows—three different solutions to the same problem in the same area from three different cultures. Each sees their solution as the right one, and are usually unwilling to consider another culture's answers. It's as if three men are looking at a rainbow; one insists that it's red, another says it's blue, while the third is certain that it's yellow. They're all partly correct, but each describes it according to his own pattern of seeing.

What is it that determines what a culture can "see"? There are ideas that lie behind the culture patterns. These ideas tell people what the world is like, who is to be obeyed, how the clouds are controlled, and what value to place upon people, animals, and rocks. These ideas come from the thinking and searching of humans to understand what's happening. They learn the accumulated knowledge and interpretations of their elders. These shared ideas from their culture determine what they see and then how they respond.

Some culture patterns are easily changed because the old patterns no longer meet today's needs. Tomorrow those patterns may change again as the situation changes. However, other patterns change very slowly. Some beliefs survive no matter how much pressure is brought to force change. Change seems to happen unpredictably, even irrationally.

Immigrants to the United States soon adopt American dress habits, but retain their distinctive hierarchical family structures. The wearing of jeans has spread from the West Coast of the USA to Japan, Germany, England, and many other countries—among certain age groups. But the use of jeans doesn't change attitudes toward America—often a mixture of anti-Americanism, desire for the American way of life, and fear of America's power. Tourists discover new tastes in food, and proudly show their "experience" by serving it to guests in their home town. At the same time, they continue with a strong belief that everything American is "number one." How can such contradictions or inconsistencies in a culture be understood?

Four Levels of Culture

It's helpful to consider different levels of culture to understand why cultures can appear to change rapidly, while at the same time there's really no basic transformation. The visible patterns of behavior are constantly being modified, often propelled by pressures from outside. But even when outside pressure is heavy, any changes in a culture's basic beliefs and assumptions will occur only slowly and incrementally.

This model of culture suggests four primary levels of culture—behavior, authority, experience, and core. (The core may also be referred to as the culture's *worldview*; the term *core* will be used here for brevity.) There are no sharp divisions between each of the levels: behavior blends into authority, acceptance of authority blends into experience, and the central core affects all levels.

We commonly refer to this model as the "cultural onion," emphasizing a culture's multilayer nature—like the layers of an onion (there are other analogies as well). Peeling away the onion's outer layers to better understand it produces tears, as does thorough learning of another culture. An onion's deeper layers are thicker and juicier and have more food value than the thin skin. Likewise in the cultural onion, a culture's deeper layers have greater influence on that culture's nature, and more significantly affect behaviors and beliefs.

The reproductive life of the onion is in the core, shown in its development of the growing tip. Similarly, patterns of living are developed from the core (or heart) of a culture.

Since growth and reproduction come from the core, change in the culture must begin with change at the core.

Four clusters of culture levels are discussed briefly below. Three of those levels include further divisions within them, which we'll name and briefly describe.

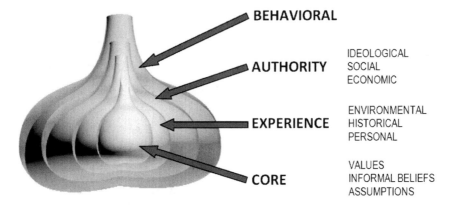

BEHAVIORAL

AUTHORITY
IDEOLOGICAL
SOCIAL
ECONOMIC

EXPERIENCE
ENVIRONMENTAL
HISTORICAL
PERSONAL

CORE
VALUES
INFORMAL BELIEFS
ASSUMPTIONS

Behavior

This is the visible level of culture—people's behaviors and objects used. This behavior layer includes the twelve languages of culture discussed in Chapters 10 and 11. These culture components can be heard and seen, recorded and measured. But recording, counting, and measuring doesn't tell us *why* people act the way they do, or why different groups in the same environment and situation act quite differently. The answer lies in the cultural layers lying beneath the visible.

Authority

Immediately beneath the behavior level are the cultural authorities. Most behavior rests on standards maintained by a culture's acknowledged authorities. At times the authorities are visible; at other times they're unwritten, unstated, and invisible—but still controlling.

The *ideological authority* is the consciously stated and taught belief system commonly accepted in a culture. It may be stated in written documents, in rituals, or in stories told to teach the young. The ideological authority may be clearly religious, as in Hinduism, Islam, or Christianity, or it may be a philosophical system as with Humanism, Rationalism, and Existentialism. The Constitution of the United States is a nonreligious ideological authority that undergirds American democracy.

It may be *social authority* that says, for instance, that farming should be done only by using a hoe. The group may be the authority prescribing that women wear dresses and men wear trousers, or perhaps the group says that people should wear nothing at all. A young person may consider himself a Christian because his family and community is Christian; his practice of Christianity rests on the authority of the group. If he changes groups, he may also apparently change his beliefs. He's really changing only the authority he acknowledges, because his beliefs are not personal but group-based.

Most individual behavior rests on social authority. When behavior changes are desirable, the primary group—and not just the individual member of a group—should be the target of change. We're all participants in a primary group and in one or more secondary groups.

Economic authority takes many forms. Obviously it applies to the gaining and spending of money. In subsistence societies, dominant economic patterns may center around the exchange of goods or services, rather than the exchange of tokens (money) representing them. An "economy of affection" may prevail, in which goods are given to create or strengthen interpersonal relationships. The "potlatch" practiced traditionally among the First Nations of northwest North American coastal regions distributed valuable goods as exchange for status position. The giving away of large quantities of valuables seemed to impoverish the giver, but in exchange he or she gained significant status—a worthwhile "economic" exchange.[13]

Economic systems based on cash exchange have different goals. In a capitalistic society, the amassing of wealth in the form of money or money equivalents brings status and power. Individualism dominates society. In a socialist system, emphasis is on distribution of wealth equally among all members of the group. Collectivism is the pattern of society. These differences are major determinants of behavior, shaping cultures in very different forms than those dominated by an economy of affection. There are many variants of economic authorities. The form prevalent in each society must be understood to progress toward a deep understanding of that group.

A striking example of misunderstanding these systemic economic differences occurred after European settlers (from capitalist systems) gained governmental control over the First Nations. They banned the potlatch as wasteful and hurtful to those who practiced it. Instead of helping, this ban destroyed an important element of First Nations' culture, contributing to cultural disintegration.

Experience

Even deeper is the collective experience of a cultural group. Again, there are three major components in this cluster of the cultural onion, each progressively more significant in shaping behavior, but in an invisible manner.

Environment shapes the ways developed to stay alive— obviously a fundamental need! Survival presents different needs in a semi-arid or arid environment, in a fertile, well-watered valley, or in a densely populated city. A person born and growing up in a great city such as Hong Kong or Cairo cannot possibly relate to the land in the same way as the person from a village along the Nile, where crops are grown in every month of the year, or in the lush but crowded Yellow

River basin of China. Neither the urban dweller nor the farmer on rich agricultural land can grasp the demands faced by the nomads of harsh deserts. These environmental differences inevitably modify culture patterns, leading to substantial differences even where they live in the same nation, speak the same language, and hold the same religious beliefs. Culture isn't determined solely by environment, but it is greatly influenced by it.

History is collective memory that deeply affects current choices and the forming of culture patterns. The history of a people hugely impacts their present, and even how they prepare for their future. To put it another way, the past is present. What happened in the past shapes what is happening now, and though invisible, the memory of what happened—or what the people believe happened—shapes today's attitudes and beliefs.

The tragedy of the Crusades shows powerfully how history shapes contemporary cultural attitudes. In Western nations, "crusade" simply means a strong and determined effort to reach a goal; the historical actions of the West in sending armies to gain control of the Holy Land happened nearly one thousand years ago is regrettably forgotten. But those "ancient" events actively shape the resentment of Islamic nations toward the West *today*. Christian organizations have used "crusade" in their names and for specific campaigns, arousing considerable suspicion of their motives in major parts of the world.

It isn't possible to understand contemporary Africa without knowing the two-hundred-year history of African-European interactions, and the legalization of racist practices in the fifty years of apartheid South Africa. Right and wrong are lost in the tangle of conquest, betrayal, and exploitation—from all parties. Today's responses are conditioned by the old stories, remembered generation after generation.

Personal experience is the most critical element for bringing change to a culture. Change begins with an individual. The individual's experience is filtered through layers of culture, colored and shaped by each layer. Though clarified or distorted by this inevitable filtering, it's still the individual's own experience, relied upon as such. What *I* have experienced, what *I* know—this I depend on.

I've found that a cup of strong, hot tea is cooling on sultry, hot days. Friends have tried to persuade me that this isn't so—but I know it's true, because I've experienced the cooling relief of hot tea again and again. My personal experience is stronger than peer pressure. That's also true in more serious matters.

I'm confident of the truth of the Bible, not from apologetic arguments or stirring sermons; I know it from personal experience. For example, how can I have restful internal peace? In Philippians 4 we're instructed, "Don't worry about anything." That's a great idea, but how do I stop worrying in a crisis? The passage continues: "Instead, pray about everything. Tell God what you need, and thank him for all he has done. Then you will experience God's peace, which exceeds anything we can understand" (Philippians 4:6-7, NLT). That is true! I know, because I've prayed and God has kept His promise. Someone can explain it some other way, or doubt my experience, but because it's *my personal* experience, I know it's true. I'm beyond persuasion or doubting about this.

Personal experience is the open window to change. The window can also be closed from earlier bad experiences. Nevertheless, reaching through the layers of culture to this window is a major key to change.

Core
The very core or heart of a culture is composed of three elements—values, informal beliefs, and assumptions.

Together they're the fundamental influences on behavior, expressed through the experience and authority levels of culture.

Values. The standards held and the principles to be maintained are the *values* that guide our actions and decisions. Some values are universal, but most differ from culture to culture, and of course, within the same culture. People seldom give thought to their values; nevertheless they're consciously or unconsciously guided by the desires that grow out of those values.

A sportsman may say he enjoys the game and plays it for sheer enjoyment. But his values of competitiveness and being the best may drive him to excess, risking injury or alienating friends.

Fairness and justice are highly valued in many societies, while other groups more highly esteem power and domination. A leader often stresses that the highest value is to be of service to the people, but first ensures that he's "on top" and has a staff that will do exactly what he considers best (often best for himself).

True values are shown in actions. In American airports, recorded announcements repeatedly proclaim, "Your safety is our highest priority." The message is replayed so often that the value seems only words, rather than alertness to real dangers.

It has been reported in research literature that there are only thirty-six different values. Those thirty-six are common to all cultures, though they're ranked differently. The highest ranking value in one culture may well be only number twenty in another. Even if all human values are present, the importance of each differs greatly from culture to culture.

Through extensive research in more than fifty nations, Geert Hofstede developed value profiles showing how each of these nations builds its way of life around 1) power distance, 2) uncertainty avoidance, 3) masculinity versus femininity, 4) individualism, 5) time orientation, and 6) indulgence versus restraint. These profiles show various implications in a useful way, and often provide a basis for comparing yet un-researched societies with those included in his studies.[14]

Informal Beliefs. Lying even deeper in culture are *informal beliefs* that are the basis of many attitudes and actions. They're called "informal" because they're often vague, unstructured, and unarticulated. They may be based on accurate fact, but expressed through superstition and vague impressions. Nevertheless, these strongly held beliefs drive surprising personal and group reactions to unfamiliar people and situations.

There's no factual physical basis for scorning a particular racial group, or considering them immoral, violent, or less intelligent. But racism exists in all parts of the world, with racial stereotypes that cause resentment and rejection, even hatred and killings. In the eighteenth and nineteenth centuries, racism saturated the so-called pacification campaigns in Asia and Africa by Western powers. It was made government policy in the apartheid period of South Africa. Even though apartheid (separate "development") was abolished in 1994, the attitudes that created it persist.

Racism shows in so-called tribalism, which is simply the select in-group against those not part of "us." It was tragically shown in Kenya's 2008 post-election violence. The disturbances quickly escalated beyond political-economic issues to the killing of those from a resented tribal group—even when they had lived together peacefully for forty or more years. Sad examples of racism and tribalism are seen worldwide, driven by informal beliefs about others who are somehow different.

Informal beliefs are prevalent, often with damaging consequences: "Women are inferior to men"; "Christians drink blood and are immoral and violent"; "All Muslims are terrorists." It's can even be "politically incorrect" to mention these beliefs, yet they contribute greatly to attitudes that create rejection, violence, and wars.

Persistent belief in the efficacy of charms and curses, the diviner's ability to discern the truth, and athletes who insist on wearing "lucky socks" to help them win are all examples of informal beliefs. These convictions may be verified by coincidences, but they usually lack objective supporting evidence. Nevertheless, they're powerful contributors to individual and cultural practices.

It can be dangerous to ignore strong informal beliefs and dismiss all of them as mere ignorance and superstition. A North American expert on poisonous frogs went to the deeper areas of the Amazon Basin in South America in search of a species never seen before. Local Indians took him to the habitat of such a frog. The Indians clearly would not touch the frogs, and cautioned the American that it was dangerous to touch them. The American ignored their warnings, picked up frogs – and was dead within a year from liver failure.

Many informal beliefs develop from familiarity—for example, food choices. Nutritional values and calories don't explain the strong preference of Asian cultures for rice as their staple, or Italian fondness for pasta, or the desire of some Africans for "mealiemeal" (white corn meal) and the insistence of others on yams or dura (millet). All are good foods—but that doesn't explain the attitude often expressed: "If I haven't had rice (or mealiemeal or yams), I haven't eaten!"

Informal beliefs may be quickly apparent, such as in acceptable foods or medical treatments, but they're often hidden and even unconscious—until a crisis calls on a culture's resources.

Assumptions

"Everyone" knows certain things to be true—that is, "everyone" in a particular cultural grouping. These things aren't subject to argument or correction; they're basic "truths." These are the basis for all parts of a culture, affecting every level of life.

Assumptions include each culture's basic ideas about:

- the nature of God
- the nature of the universe
- the nature of mankind
- the nature of reality
- relationships between God, the universe, and humanity
- how we know

These assumptions influence what we choose to see and do, and how we interpret everything. They're the foundation on which culture is built. Or to change the metaphor, they're the colored windows through which we see the world. If the glasses are green, the world will appear green. No amount of argument will convince us that the color red exists, since it can be seen only as black when looking through green glasses.

Assumptions are usually not consciously held;[15] they're acquired from the time of birth through enculturation—the learning process by which we become functional members of our culture.

In countless gestures, in words, and in all of communication, babies learn about the world—life, God, and the nature of things. Normally this creed cannot even be adequately expressed, partly because it hasn't been consciously learned. That which has been learned without words is very difficult to express with words. The core is nevertheless strong, very resistant to change, and the controlling element in shaping a life. It's the core that determines what the person can even perceive out of the massive number of stimuli received.

To a considerable degree, assumptions determine what personal experience we have and what groups have authority over us, and consequently how we outwardly behave. They're like a building's foundation. If the foundation is square, the building will be square. If there's a curve in the foundation, then the building's wall will curve. The shape and even size of the completed building is determined by the foundation beneath. Once the building is built, it's impossible to change the foundation without smashing down the building.

Chapter Thirteen

The Critical Component—The Core

How does the "cultural onion" model of culture relate to behavior and change?

Let's consider the growth of Christian belief in a child. When very young, the baby attempts to follow the practices and example of his parents. He imitates their outward actions, their behavioral level of culture. The child learns to fold hands, to say the words of a prayer, and to sing simple songs. He learns how to act and what to expect at times of celebration such as Christmas and Easter. As he grows older, he knows how to act like a Christian.

At the same time, he's watching and learning the attitudes of older people toward Christian faith. Though largely unconscious, the child learns what is valued and what is merely surface behavior.

In all children, there comes a time of curiosity about the actions observed and the beliefs that have been taught. Questions are asked, and are answered by people in authority—parents, pastor, teachers. Being "Christian" has moved from the behavioral level to the authority level of culture. "My father told me," or "The pastor said so" is enough to confirm belief because the authority of those people is acknowledged.

As the child grows, a conflict often emerges as authorities gradually change. The peer group reduces family importance as the authority to be followed. In the teenage years the peer group is often a stronger authority than the family and church. Peer group authority often leads to changes in outward actions, and a youth may no longer act like a Christian. If the peer group is strongly supportive of the Christian message, then entering the teen years may mean a deepening of Christian practice.

At this point a more powerful authority may be accepted, leading to a personal experiencing of the life of Christ. Prayer becomes intimate. Obeying Scripture becomes enjoyable. Those who respond personally to Christ's invitation to follow Him soon discover that He does give rest and fulfillment. In short, they experience for themselves something that had been accepted only on the basis of authority.

Beliefs based on personal experience are very difficult to change. "I know" is much stronger than "he told me." Others may laugh and say that belief is nothing, but if the reality of Christ is personally experienced, Christian commitment will be strongly held. Commitment based on personal experience will not be easily changed.

The way in which Christian experience is expressed is influenced by the cultural core. If the culture's core includes concern for strangers, people will probably become active in relief efforts or caring for the poor. If arts and music are valued, Christian experience may be expressed in beautiful sanctuaries and rich music. Each culture can contribute uniquely to the richness of the Christian church around the world.

Core values, informal beliefs, and assumptions are not changed by discussion or by reasoning. They lie too deeply to be altered by a forced change in behavior. It's difficult to discuss beliefs held at the core because a contrary view is inconceivable. If a person is faced with another position, the polite reaction is to laugh. If the alternate position is insisted upon, anger may arise. If even anger doesn't stop this foolish, contrary idea, then the idea must be treated with mockery and scorn. When even that fails, the idea and the messenger of the idea are considered a threat that must be destroyed. At best, challenging the core leads to disregard. At the extreme, challenging the core leads to the challenger's death.

Is it ever possible to change the core? The core is developed through enculturation, by which a baby becomes a responsible adult member of society. It follows that the only way the core can be changed is for the person to once again become a "baby." That's precisely what Jesus Christ said: "You must be born again." It's significant that the terms *new birth, born again,* and *becoming as a little child* are used in regard to Christian commitment. It's in this way that Christian belief can change the patterns of individual lives and of cultures. The social and psychological problem of changing deeply held attitudes and behavior patterns has a theological answer.

Some Different Core Beliefs

The whole idea of core beliefs (sometimes referred to as existential postulates) may be easier to understand after contrasting core beliefs concerning the same things in two different culture groups, African and European.

African cultures typically regard the world as something like an organism. No sharp distinction is made between materials. The distinction between organic and inorganic is according to the strength of spirit power or vital force that everything possesses to some degree. This spirit power, or life essence, permeates everything we see—rocks, trees, animals, mountains. People have this spirit power as well. The actions of people are controlled by these powers, both for good and bad. Power and protection for the individual depend upon proper respect and manipulation of these forces.

In contrast, Western cultures view the world as a machine. It has no feelings, and is lifeless even though it has motion. Cutting a road into a mountain may unfortunately cause erosion, but that has no consequences beyond the movement of soil in an undesirable way. A rock may be blasted apart, rivers may be dammed, trees can be burned, and animals can be shot. As long as these things aren't destroyed completely, preventing future generations from benefiting from them, it's completely correct to do those things. The world is here for man to exploit. It has no feeling, there's no power in it beyond the physical laws that control it. A machine is to be understood, kept in good operating condition, and used to benefit the operator of the machine. Man operates the machine called earth.

These two opposing beliefs are so deeply held that the Westerner finds it almost impossible to understand African belief in spirit forces of the world. Controlling those spirit forces seems sheer superstition and nonsense to the Westerner. He has no fear of damming the river because he doesn't recognize spirit power in that river. Change of farming methods, new practices in childbirth or in disease control have no meaning to him beyond their usefulness in operating the world machine more satisfactorily. The African, however, considers these as changes affecting the critical balance in the spirit world, possibly leading to unexpected disasters.

Discussion of these things often doesn't help, but may cause distrust and even anger between two groups having such different assumptions about the world.

When core beliefs are being challenged—proceed with great caution!

Limited or Unlimited Good?

A basic belief in Western cultures is that there is unlimited good in the world. There can be constant improvement, leading to a higher and higher standard of living for everyone. If one person or one group is able to improve their crops for a higher yield, that's considered good, and others seek to imitate it. Everyone may gain a better crop by using a superior method. Whenever one person's hard work brings an increase in standard of living, this takes nothing away from anyone else, since there's the possibility of unlimited good. All that needs to be done is for other people to learn the superior method to also improve their standard of living.

However, many cultures believe there's only limited good in this world. If one group raises its standard of living, it does so by taking something away from someone else. When group one raises its standard of living, it prevents other groups from also raising their standard of living, because that good has already been taken. There is less available to use. People who assume limited good don't think they could imitate wealthier nations and thereby raise their own standard of living. Instead there's the feeling that the wealthy have taken more than their share of the limited good, and so have exploited those who don't have as much.

Recognizing the difference in these basic beliefs—between unlimited good and limited good—helps us understand why many in the poorer nations of the southern hemisphere blame nations of the northern hemisphere for exploiting them. The Northerners find that hard to understand; after all, they're operating development and aid programs. Their people are giving away their skills, medicine, and food. They deny taking anything from the people, but instead point out that they're sharing what's rightfully theirs from good thinking and hard work. According to their basic beliefs, they certainly aren't taking anything from the people.

But impoverished Southerners[16] don't think that way. They probably cannot tell you why they feel resentful, or why they agree with the charges of exploitation. Nevertheless, emotionally they feel that the Northerners are exploiting rather than helping them. They may not see the exploitation visibly, but the very fact that the Northerner has so much and they have so little establishes that the Northerners dipped too deeply into the pool of limited good.

No Separate Compartments

There are, of course, many other differences at the core of African and European cultures. It's essential to at least attempt to learn the core beliefs of the people with whom we work. If we don't understand the core beliefs, our well-planned agricultural or medical programs will get nowhere. Instead, they may create hostility that leads to failure and rejection.[17]

A common assumption in outside Europe and North America is that all of life is one. Secular and sacred are the same. Religion links with all of life, and is not a separate activity, as in the European pattern. So in a very real sense, religion controls the activities of life. For example, certain river pools are the dwelling of spirits. If you were to wash in that pool at the wrong season of the year, you would offend the spirit of the pool. Such beliefs about the supernatural affect daily living.

Another example of this unified approach to life—often referred to as holism—is in the Islamic approach to government and religion. Religion and government aren't separated in their core, but are part of the same thing—how do we live our *whole* life. Most Secular societies of the West insist on strict separation of the state from any religious activity. Religion in the West is often neatly separated into a Sunday performance. Even where there's a state church, it's often disregarded in political decisions and daily life.

At times, people may decline to do something that we ask, and we can learn no reason for the refusal. Behind the rebuff, there's usually a different assumption about how the world operates. We need to dig deeper to find out why the rejection is there.

Among South Sudan's Lotuho, certain drums are considered to have very potent spirit power. The essence of the power of the village is considered to be in the drum. Whenever drums must be repaired, the work is done with ceremony and great care so that the spirits won't be offended.

Water is frequently treated with great reverence in non-Western societies. Be very careful before insisting upon any scheme involving water, even if Western science says it is right. Strongly held beliefs may underlie resistance to the proposed scheme.

People or Things?

In European cultures, things and ideas tend to be given greater importance than people. This is usually not admitted; in fact, leaders often repeat that people are what count. However, the words of Ecclesiastes may well apply: "The more the words, the less the meaning" (Ecclesiastes 6:11). Many words say that people are important, but vigorous denials may really indicate the truth of the charge! Things and ideas tend to dominate people in Western cultures.

Watch what happens in an African home when a child breaks a cup. It's more or less ignored. In many American homes, the child would usually be promptly admonished, and the child quickly learns that it's very bad to break things. The assumption in African life is that good relationships must be maintained within the community at all costs. Bad relationships are a very serious matter, and may be the cause of sickness or lack of rainfall. A broken cup is much less important than a broken relationship.

When there is sickness or a problem, Africans and many Asian peoples generally are more concerned with some relational cause for how it came about, rather some scientific or medical explanation. Bad relationships with people or departed ancestors result in trouble. The common core belief is that people relationships are primary. Questions of inoculations and fertilizers are secondary.

Therefore, maintaining good people relationships takes priority over things. That doesn't mean there are never bad relationships in African and Asian societies; however, basic belief compels attempts to first heal any relationships that are broken. Living in harmony with your village and clan is part of the way to assure health and prosperity.

Westerners typically want scientific explanations for poor rain, sickness, or the poor economy—everything must be explained. How it happened is important; any underlying relational cause is less important. The weather patterns are unfavorable, it is said, and a full scientific explanation is given. The reason why a particular weather pattern occurred is usually explained by another series of "how" answers. In the case of an epidemic, how the disease is transmitted may be explained. Why it began is of less importance, so answers are seldom attempted, except in general terms such as genetics, or an unknown virus, or perhaps just bad luck. Elsewhere, peoples are often more concerned with "why" and may seek the answer with diviners and fortune-tellers.

Are Cities Different?

Visiting the great cities of the Majority World overwhelms the Westerner—so many people, so much activity on the streets, creative entrepreneurs and numbing poverty side by side, great wealth and power held by a few, limited ways to physically improve life. Does the cultural onion model apply in such places?

These cities are marked not only by the mixing of wealth and poverty, but also by a seething potpourri of cultures and languages, clans and tribes, castes and outcasts, the internationally educated and the functionally illiterate, world travelers sitting in churches with the many who have never left the area where they were born. It's unlikely that the flow of people to Majority World cities will stop or even be slowed in the near future. *World* magazine points out, "More than half of the world's population lives in cities now, but by 2050 more than 70 percent will. China, India, and Africa will be leading the way." Meanwhile, in just the next two decades, "400 million Chinese and 215 million Indians will move to urban areas, more than the population of the U.S. and Brazil combined."[18]

Mission must refocus on cities, shifting from primary concern for rural areas from which the population is draining, especially the men and the young adults. Rural regions must not be ignored, but neither must we overlook the turbulent concentrations with unfamiliar challenges.

Since it's the purpose to reach and transform the core, what is the core of city cultures? Is it the same for city-dwellers as it was when they were in rural villages?

Outwardly many things have changed. The role of the husband and father is different than it was in rural home areas. No longer does he meet family needs by his own hard work in farming or hunting and gathering, nor does he need to be the warrior defending his family from raiders and rogue animals. How can he provide for his family? There's very often no family nearby to help. Where does he find work and earn money when his abilities are suited for an entirely different economy?

The wife doesn't have a garden, and relatives are no longer part of her daily life. She doesn't need to spend hours carrying water; it's nearby, or even inside the house. There's no place to gather fuel for her cooking fire, and perhaps they don't have or cannot pay for other fuels. She must learn new skills to feed and clothe her family with money instead of by her labor.

There's no single "core" for city-dwellers, even in the same city. Similarities exist, however, between many of the now-urban groups, even where outer levels of culture have sharply changed. The approach to the core is different, but the core itself changes only very slowly. Change is measured over generations rather than the years of a single life. So it's useful to understand the traditional core, recognizing that the way it's expressed through the experience, authority, and behavior levels of culture will be changed.

Change in culture is not at a constant rate throughout. Some more visible parts change rapidly and perhaps often, while deeper levels change more slowly. The rate of culture change is something like a spinning bicycle wheel—the outer rim moves most rapidly, while the motion at the wheel's center near the hub is slower.

There is much that changes for people who move or are moved from areas where their tribe and families have lived for many generations—perhaps for centuries—but the core remains constant. Behavior changes speedily, to make necessary adaptations to a new environment and new models of behavior.

Authority that controls life is different, often younger, speaking different languages and demanding different actions and loyalties. Experience changes much more slowly. The environment is very different, forcing change. But that change is slowed by the memories and practices of thought embedded in history of the family, tribe, and home area. Those change only as new experiences create new memories and new attitudes.

No longer can family, clan, and village essentially determine personal actions. The nuclear family must develop its own ways in adjustment to the unknown urban environment. Their personal experience has become the living, learning edge of life. It's the "open window" through which previously rejected ideas are considered, from behaviors to even values and informal beliefs. Though changes are considered, the deeper levels of culture still change very slowly—creating anomalies and contradictions between "modern" behavior and the continuing core.

Assumptions are so deeply held that it's pointless to ask who's right and who's wrong. It's a matter of what is believed, and what is assumed to be correct. We must work with those assumptions instead of arguing with them, or worse, working within only our own basic assumptions. Until the different assumptions held by people are understood and addressed, progress will be slow and significant change will not occur.

These very different core beliefs affect Christian ministry directly. The practical result is that goals must be reached by different paths in different cultures. A pattern for mission developed in the West can seldom be transferred fruitfully anywhere in the Majority World—wearing jeans doesn't make an American, nor does it ensure that an American response will result.

God loves every person and every culture. The least we can do is show respect to people and their culture by working from "inside," patiently learning how their entire culture functions—from behavior through to their assumptions. This is true incarnational ministry—the exhibition of the life of Jesus within every level of a culture.

PART FIVE

Stimulating Change

We've learned that positive change is not imported into a culture; it is stimulated. The culture controls the change. The outsider who wants to be a deliberate change agent must move slowly in close cooperation with the society's insiders. More is required than good intentions, and more than a knowledge of the group and its culture. An effective strategy must be followed.

The next four chapters introduce some of the most basic considerations in developing that strategy.

Chapter Fourteen

Helping Where Help Is Wanted

Where do we begin? The list of needs is endless. Better water, more food, adequate health care, improving the schools, building the roads, and seeking to introduce new ways to meet needs and to earn cash. A long list of things that people need to be given for "development" is easy to make. All the items on the list are of genuine importance. Yet which items come first?

Is it most important to give a clean and constantly available water supply? What good is a water supply if there's not enough food to get through the dry season? What good are all these things if a raid from a neighboring tribe captures the cattle and kills some of the people? Or in a different setting, why improve housing in an urban slum if there's no way to earn money to buy food for the family? Improved preaching seems irrelevant when churchgoers may be beaten or robbed on their way home.

Where is help needed—and especially, where is it wanted?

The problem of development is like trying to find the beginning of a perfect circle. Every need is related to every other need, each depending upon the other. Without all needs being met, there won't be genuine development. Meeting health needs makes us more aware of the need for a better food supply, and that makes us aware of the need to change farming methods. But farming methods are closely linked to values derived from traditional religious beliefs. Changed religious beliefs will create a desire for education in many cases, a desire that cannot be met without more cash. Introducing the beginnings of a cash economy may destroy the traditional cooperative social structure of the tribe. Interdependencies like these are there in every setting.

Every need leads to another, and every change leads to other changes. So which is the right place to begin introducing change?

Change can best be introduced by beginning with the felt needs of the people. It's not nearly as important to meet "the most important" need as it is to meet those needs which the people themselves feel are important. In meeting these felt needs, a basis for trust is built up. That trust is necessary for meeting the next needs, and the next needs after that.

It's hard to believe that people who aren't technologically developed can know what their needs are. It's a great temptation for people from a materially strong culture to decide what other people need. But even with strong technology, outsiders cannot know as much about the land as those who have lived on the land for generations. And if you haven't personally dwelt in an urban slum with its often vibrant way of life, how can you tell the people there how they must change and improve their existence?

It's valuable to recognize three different kinds of needs— *felt, perceived,* and *real.*

Felt needs are those which the people themselves are aware of. When they ask for help, they'll ask for a particular need. They recognize what they want and are looking for a way to obtain it.

Perceived needs are what the outsider sees as important. He's not as emotionally part of the scene as insiders are—a fact he views as being to his advantage. He feels he can more objectively analyze the problem and determine where help should begin; he expects to use his knowledge and skills to identify the truly important problems, and then begin working on them.

But his perception of the most important needs doesn't really matter if the people inside the culture don't agree. The insiders will simply not pay attention to him, and they may even hinder the outsider's efforts to introduce what he feels are necessary changes. It doesn't matter if the outsider is technically "correct"; it's the insider's life that's involved. It's his people, his cattle, his safety; there's no reason why he should change because someone he doesn't know tells him he should.

We do need to identify the *real needs*—but that can never be done by the insider *or* the outsider acting alone. Each can contribute something to the continuing discussion that will define real needs. The insider obviously knows the problem most adequately. It's also the insider's own understanding and determination that will decide the effectiveness of any change introduced. But the outsider brings new possibilities. He has seen different answers to similar problems in other places. He usually has technical skills to find answers that couldn't be found by the insider alone.

Nevertheless, the outsider must never disregard the considerable technical skills developed by the insider specifically to meet local conditions. Those skills are often of much greater value than they seem at first glance. A simple example of undetected skills happened in a village of the Congo Basin in the center of Africa. An outsider wanted to improve the yield of their crops, so he insisted that they stop raising the crop areas into small rectangles a foot or more above the rest of the land. He demonstrated how his method was much easier, planting in rows level with surrounding land. But when the annual rains began, the land was inundated with water flooding and destroying his crops. But crops of those who continued in the traditional way were above the small floods. Their crops not only survived, but benefited from the water.

When an outsider comes to help, he must first be prepared to listen to the felt needs and thoroughly understand them. He can then, in a relationship of trust, suggest other ways to meet other needs and be ready for modifications from the insider before a new idea is tried. Together, by discussion and trial, the real needs can be understood and then met.

All three needs—felt, real, perceived—are important. They are three different stages of the long and often difficult journey of change and development. Felt needs by themselves often give an incomplete picture. Perceived needs are frequently superficial and overlook important problems that the insider sees. The real need can seldom be directly identified, and thus must be approached through understanding both the felt and perceived needs in discussion that builds trust between groups.

In other words, constructive change cannot occur until we know the needs as the people themselves view them. Attempting to force change before understanding felt needs will create resistance, thus blocking genuine progress for a long time to come instead of speeding it up.

We're working with an audience that is active, not passive. People are not a blackboard on which you can write anything you wish; rather, they're involved with you in considering whatever you're trying to change. The people demand something from this communication. If it doesn't meet their need, they're not going to be interested in what you have to say. The people will select from your words only that which they see as useful to them. Other ideas that don't seem useful will be ignored. What *you* consider to be most important doesn't matter.

All human attention is highly selective. We listen only to the things that seem important or interesting to us. If we don't think something is of much value, we simply don't pay attention. If the people we're working with don't think our suggestions are useful or important, they're simply not going to perceive what we say. They "turn it off," often not even recalling that we seriously made a suggestion.

Considering communication primarily as a matter of technique is to miss a key point. Good communication techniques may attract attention at the beginning, but content won't be remembered unless it helps meet some felt need.

We see that in our churches. A good preacher may keep people's attention during the service, yet afterward the congregation cannot tell what the preacher really said. Rightly or wrongly, they regarded the sermon as irrelevant to their needs, so the message is disregarded.

In communication we're operating in a free marketplace, where the buyer takes only what he wants and pays only the price he thinks the item is worth. People will listen only to that which seems important, and will remember and apply the information only if it seems of value in their own lives.

Behavior that has produced desirable results in the past will not be quickly changed, even under outside pressure. A culture pattern that satisfies people's needs will be continued. The suggestions and instructions of a development agent, a government worker, or a missionary will not lead people to change something that seems satisfactory to them.

It's amazing, for example, to see the steep slopes on which South Sudan's Didinga people grow their crops. There's no terracing used to stop soil erosion and hold the water on the steep fields. As population increases, more and more soil is lost from the steep slopes. More trees are cut, more brush is cleared, and water runs off more rapidly. In a few years, the fertile Didinga hills will become less productive. Malnutrition will increase, and even outright starvation will result.

As an outsider, I would like to teach the Didinga about terracing their fields, but there's no indication they feel any need to learn that skill and to do that vast amount of work. Their present way of farming is giving them food, and by farming in several fields at different altitudes in the hills, they seem to always have some kind of crop. There's no felt need to change their style of agriculture. Their present farming methods have been successful for many generations, so there's little possibility that change will come soon.

Introduction of pit latrines has been almost totally unsuccessful in the villages of Eastern Equatoria in South Sudan. Why has there been so much resistance to this change in sanitation methods? The present waste disposal method seems to work satisfactorily. A problem is seldom seen because the bush area around each village is still large. The climate of heavy rains and intense sun, plus plant life and natural scavengers like dung beetles and birds, seem to take care of the problem.

Though health care workers explain how infection is spread because of poor waste disposal, it's hard to actually see this correlation. The pattern of many generations is still working today. There's little felt need for a different way of waste disposal, except in crowded town areas. The people have survived with the old methods. Therefore there's little reason to change those old patterns.

In agriculture, there are many possible changes that could increase food production. If new concepts such as ox-plowing, crops in rows, and rotation of crops with new varieties were all adopted, food production would increase many times. Instead of being an area constantly on the edge of famine, Eastern Equatoria could become an area to export food. But is there any felt need to export food on the part of the people? Do they themselves feel any need to plant in rows? What difference would the use of plows make in their food supply? If they had more food, would it not simply be eaten by rats and termites?

Even if the people are persuaded that these changes would help meet their deepest felt need for regular food supplies, they'll be very slow to change. After all, their fathers and grandfathers and great-grandfathers planted for generations without using rows or oxen or new crop varieties, and they survived. The old patterns are still meeting fundamental felt needs, at least to some degree.

There's a felt need for preventing measles epidemics, and the people have quite quickly accepted the measles vaccine. This has been demonstrated to be better than traditional ways, so there's now widespread acceptance of this change brought by health care workers.

Felt needs are the beginning point for change. To begin the process of development in spiritual, economic, or social areas of life, first identify what people say are their needs. Try to understand those needs from the community's viewpoint, then seek ways to meet those needs as directly as possible—and in full cooperation with the people, so they can see how the things you're doing with them will answer their needs.

It may be that the felt need is not the most important need, nor what you would consider their real need. But by meeting that need cooperatively, the essential bridge of trust is built between yourself as change agent and the people you've come to help. Short step by short step, you and the people will work more deeply into the problems of the community until the basic needs, the real needs, are being met. Meanwhile, in this lengthy process, you'll have increased the community's ability to solve its own problems. They'll be less dependent on outside help so they can maintain their own self-respect.

The people can be forced to change, of course, by use of outside pressure. That pressure could be military occupation, or it could be relief programs giving food and other benefits in return for the people doing jobs that the outside agency determines are important. Charity can be just as powerful as guns in bringing change, and equally destructive.

Force can bring change very rapidly, but it's almost always shallow. As soon as force is removed, people go back to doing things as they did them before. The change isn't voluntary, and it often makes people dependent upon the outside force. When the force is removed, people go back to the old ways with which they met their needs before force was applied.

It has been a frequent practice to build roads during times of famine, with food grain given in return for work on the roads. When the famine is over, the roads often deteriorate because most of the villages have little felt need for the roads. On the other hand, some new things are adopted very quickly because they meet existing felt needs. Guns have been quickly adopted because they give an advantage in cattle raiding or urban crime gangs.

The basis for beginning change can be quite simply summed up: People will genuinely change to meet their felt needs, and for no other reason. Forced change creates resentment and reaction.

What about spiritual changes? Should we wait until there's a felt need for spiritual change before we preach the gospel of Jesus Christ?

Yes. That need exists in every person. As Augustine accurately expressed it, there's a God-shaped void inside every person. Every person has a sense of need for God. When that need isn't being met, people are open to learn and change. They'll put confidence in Christ when they understands for themselves that the knowledge of Christ meets that need to know God.

Too often that deeply felt need isn't met because those who carry the good news of Christ ignore felt needs, seeking to change people's minds and hearts while overlooking what the people themselves consider important. If those from the outside had spent time discussing and working with the community to meet their felt needs, their spiritual needs could also have been met.

Bruce Olson first sought to understand the Motilone in South America when he went to them as a missionary. As he lived among them, he discovered that the people had a legend. At one time, God was among them, but then He went far away. He promised, however, that He would send them a banana stalk that would tell them the message of how to come back to Him. When Olson heard this legend, it didn't make sense. How could God speak to the people through a banana stalk? But one day he was in the bush with some of the people as they were cutting bananas. Somebody cut the bottom part of the banana plant, and then as they slashed across the top the whole banana stalk "unrolled." The leaves that were wrapped around each other spread out.

Suddenly Bruce Olson saw that it looked exactly like a book being opened. With great excitement and happiness, Olson understood. He called to the men, "I know where God's banana stalk is. I have it!" They were equally excited.

When they went back to the village that night, Olson was able to speak good news to the people from God's banana stalk, the Bible. The legend portrayed the deeply felt need to be in union with God. In being with the people, the legend was heard and then understood, and the need was met.

On the basis of that felt need being met, Olson was able to begin working with the people to meet other felt needs. New medicines were introduced through the traditional healers in the tribe. Crops were improved, and development proceeded rapidly.

When we work *with* the people, inside their culture, we act as a resource they can use. We don't tell them what they must do; we offer help that they desire. Working this way, we'll understand important details and problems in meeting the needs. Change will begin to occur, and true development will begin.

Chapter Fifteen

Change the Group

"Of course individuals are more important than the group. Individual human rights must always be protected!" Western nations are often built on that assumption. Individuals make decisions and determine the form of government and who's in power. Individuals shape their own lifestyle, and choose their own churches, friends, and jobs. Leaders seek to influence the individual as he votes. Merchants influence the individual shopper in selecting what to buy. Christian appeals are directed to individuals, whether in or out of the church. The individual is considered the basic unit in Western society—so we give priority to the individual.

In most Asian and African societies, however, the group is considered the primary unit. Therefore the group, not the individual, is the crucial place to work in bringing change.

Often, decisions about which crop to plant will be made in the group, as well as the building of a school or road, or even which church will be "accepted" for the people. The family group arranges marriage, and shares responsibility for raising the children and ensuring their education. In some group-centered societies, it's almost unthinkable for an individual to make decisions in major areas of life; those decisions are discussed in the group and reached by consensus.

The individual doesn't lose a sense of identity, however. The individual doesn't feel a speck of dust carried along by the flood, manipulated by group forces beyond individual power and understanding. In the group's concern and care, there is deep security and strong identity. To lose the group would be to lose oneself.

Recognizing the contrast with Western understandings, a common saying is, "We are...therefore I am."

Within the group, change can and does happen. The group doesn't rigidly oppose all new ideas and change; it will always try to find the best way for its members to be secure, healthy, and prosperous. The group will act in its own self-interest as it determines what would be best. In a group-oriented society, then, the group—*not* the individual—must be the primary target for bringing change.

A group-oriented society will seek to protect itself in order to preserve the group. Ideas that are unknown and untried in the group are often seen as a disturbing, threatening element that may lead to the group's disintegration—something that can never be risked. Loss of the group would mean loss of security and identity! Lacking fuller understanding, the group will reject proposed changes that remain unproven and unfamiliar.

This is a major challenge for outsiders trying to begin development or change of any kind. Change agents, whether development workers, politicians, or missionaries, are almost always *outside* the group. They stand alongside, but apart from, the group they're trying to change. Even with careful effort to introduce change, it still comes from the outside. The outsider has no standing in the group; ideas cannot be introduced *inside* the group because the outsider is not there.

An outsider with experience of the proposed change may scold the people for being too conservative and failing to see how the change will help the group. Rebels from the group may then try to adopt the change by themselves. By doing so, they further alienate themselves from their own group.

They do gain, however, the praise of outsiders for being the "only truly progressive and intelligent" group members. This brings them some advantages—for example, outside assistance and new opportunities. Their preliminary rebellion from the group is thus strengthened. Well-intended pressures to change the society instead begin the disintegration of the society.

How Can We Avoid Such Destructive "Help"?

The most far-reaching change, and the least disturbing, comes when change begins within the group, even though stimulated by outsiders. The group itself, not individuals pulled out of the group, is the place for change to occur. Discussion of the new idea is group discussion, using the normal channels for information flow and consideration. Then when decision is reached, the group acts together, supporting the individuals making changes. The strength of the group supports change; the group is made stronger and at the same time more open to considering other changes.

The best way for an outsider to begin group change is for the outsider to become an accepted member of the group. Two stories of how that can happen are told in two very different videos, *Inn of the Sixth Happiness* and *Dance With the Wolves*. The first story is of Gladys Aylward, a missionary to China,. Her story is also told in the book *The Small Woman*. The second is of an American who became part of an American Indian tribe, in the film directed by Kevin Costner. Both show that those trying to create change and the people to be changed must develop a strong sense of belonging to the *same* group. A sense of belonging to the group makes it easier to understand the issues involved because discussion is easier. Discussion leads to a better grasp of how to change. Problems are anticipated and can often be avoided as the group discusses and participates in the decision-making.

People are less defensive and suspicious of new ideas when those ideas come from within the group. The idea has a better chance of a fair hearing.

Bring Change from Within

To summarize, when bringing constructive change to a group is desirable, the change agent must be closely involved with the group. Better yet, the one bringing change and those to be changed should feel that they *belong* to the same society.

How then, can we be effective in bringing constructive change when we obviously belong to a different group?

Only a fortunate few—very few—can ever become fully accepted into the society of another people and another culture. Most of us remain outside, observers never able to fully enter into another way of life. Yet we care enough about these others to desire to help them, to strengthen them, and to share with them the best things of God and of the world He gave us. But we cannot seem to speak "loudly" enough so these others can hear. Can it ever be possible to get enough "inside" so we can start change? This is the hard part. This is the central challenge of cross-cultural communication.

Change cannot be brought by "injection." Underdevelopment isn't a sickness to be treated with a hypodermic needle of "communication." "Learn how to use communication," this false reasoning says; "fill it with the right instructions, and then give the injection."

"If the correct injection is given," some would say, "the patient doesn't need to understand. Just tell people the right thing to do, and demonstrate and teach them how to follow this better way." In other words, *inject* the message—then go on your way to help someone else. But when the injection wears off, things continue as they were before; there has been no permanent change.

"But there's no way I can be anybody else except myself," we easily protest. "I can never become a member of this group I'm trying to help. So how can I be heard *inside* this group?"

Before we continue, let's summarize our difficulties:

1. To be heard correctly inside another culture is almost impossible.

2. "Injecting" the message creates only temporary change.

3. Until the message is perceived as coming from inside the group, outside effort will not ensure a fair trial of the new idea.

Chapter Sixteen

From Inside Out

What changes a collection of individuals into a society? When individuals who don't know each other come together for any reason, some type of group organization soon emerges. Leaders develop, dependable workers emerge, and those with special knowledge are identified.

What brings this result? *Communication* that uses all twelve of the signal systems. It's the process of total communication that binds a group together, helping each member find his part in the whole. It then keeps the group distinct from other groups. Communication in the social body is like blood in the physical body. Without it, the different parts cannot function, and life is impossible.

Communication systems are developed in every society. Without participation of its members, the group cannot operate. It cannot effectively meet the needs of its members and will ultimately disintegrate.

This, for example, is what happened among the Ik people along the Uganda-Sudan border, as described by anthropologist Colin Turnbull in *The Mountain People*. Under the pressures of famine, the larger group broke down into smaller units in the effort to gain food, and those smaller units further broke down into families. Then even the families began to break apart in the terrible struggle for survival. Small groups of less than ten people isolated themselves from all others who had been members of their society. The Ik disintegrated as a separate people.

Communication hold a society together by helping individuals know how to play their role in the larger group. The rainmaker in Navajo society knows through communication with predecessors and with other rainmakers—as well as from the people's expectations—what his role is and how he can fulfill it. At gatherings of a Dogon village, the "mouth"—someone who restates everything a public speaker says—helps to guarantee understanding and reduce conflict.

Among the Toposa people, frequent meetings of the men allow discussion on subjects of interest to the village. Men's opinions are formed by discussion with others. Each man both learns from and teaches the other men so that group values of the Toposa are kept and acted upon. Women hear from their husband, and they in turn, discuss with other wives while they till the gardens or cook the meals. Curses, or the threat of curses, enforce adherence to the group patterns. In hundreds of such ways, communication ensures that each individual performs the expected social roles.

Individuals participate in the larger group through communication in at least three ways: 1) rituals, 2) discussions, and 3) sharing work.

Rituals—such as annual ceremonial hunts, homecoming events, and parades—are forms of communication that portray group values and encourage individual participation in the group. It may be the Mardi Gras festivals, famous in Rio de Janeiro, New Orleans, and other cities; or the "moment of silence" to remember fallen soldiers or the death of prominent citizens. Ritual in churches is an enactment of beliefs and the story that undergirds the church's existence, as in the rite of baptism or communion. It is powerful communication using several signal systems, bonding participants together within a group.

Discussions in a traditional consensus society not only provide a review of information before making a decision, but ensure that the ruling generation participate socially with others in that generation. Discussions within any organization increase group consciousness. Calling for help in farming activities[19] by the symbolic scattering of soil over those you're asking is communication that ensures participation in the society. The way work is divided between age groups and between men and women communicates the divisions that society wishes to maintain. All these, and hundreds of other practices, are communications that create and maintain a social grouping.

And lastly, communication is the way individuals maintain identification with the values and symbols that make a society unique. Rituals especially express these values, such as annual Toposa ceremonies featuring the sacrifice of a bull. Many societies have a ritual of thanksgiving at the end of harvest. Initiation ceremonies are a teaching form to impart values and knowledge of the secret symbols that represent those values. Ritual communication strengthens loyalties of group members and visibly separates that society from other societies.

In churches, communication is used to emphasize distinctive positions. In Baptist churches, for example, the pulpit is placed at the center front of the sanctuary to emphasize the central importance of the preaching and teaching of God's Word. In churches of Roman Catholic tradition, the altar is central and the pulpit to one side, emphasizing the importance of the altar and eucharist.

Every society has its own communication system, using the twelve signal systems in a manner unique to that society. A communication method basic in one society may be unimportant in another. To fully understand the society, it's necessary to understand its communication system. When a society's communication channels are broken and ineffective, the society itself changes and may even break apart.

Before 1970, the Turkana people of northern Kenya were one tribal unit, with lesser divisions according to clan and geographic regions. They lived as semi-nomads on the desert shores of Lake Turkana, herding goats and camels. Their prized cattle were kept on adjacent highlands. In the early 1970s a severe drought crippled their lifestyle, threatening the lives of the Turkana. To help them survive, international aid organizations and national churches taught the Turkana how to fish from the rich waters of Lake Turkana where fifty-pound perch were not uncommon. Approximately 20,000 of the Turkana came to the lake shores and learned fishing, very reluctantly at first. They survived, and the reduced population pressure enabled the other 80,000 Turkana to survive in their traditional desert way of life.

However, there was little opportunity among the fishermen for traditional Turkana ways. A life based on fishing made different demands than life based on cattle. As a result, the independent Turkana nomads wanted no part of the despised occupation of fishing. Communication between the desert dwellers and the fishing folk was disrupted. The fishing Turkana settled along the lake shore in a few communities, maintaining little contact with the desert people. The desert people continued their austere form of life; a few old men were allowed alcoholic drinks, adultery was severely punished, and friendship highly prized. The traditional desert network of communication was maintained through wedding feasts, various living crises, and funeral ceremonies. Diviners as the central figures continued to hold the people to traditional values.

At the same time, the fishing Turkana moved into a new way of life that wasn't nomadic. The sale of fish gave the foundation for a cash economy. Settlements grew, bringing people closer together than they had been on the desert.

Nothing in their culture told them how to care for resulting sanitation problems. The tribal communication network wasn't appropriate to this new setting and was unable to bind the people by continuation of traditional values. The time-honored supremacy of friendship lost its power; money became a greater power. Alcohol was available for a price, and not just to those of the right social standing. Traditional marriage arrangements no longer worked, because people didn't have large herds of livestock to exchange to bond the families of the bride and groom together. Illegitimate births rose rapidly.

What had been one tribe became in effect two tribes, even though they speak a common language. The communication networks had been pulled apart, and among the fishing people it wasn't replaced with anything that continued to hold everyone to their traditional values. Change was rapid, yet largely destructive. With the loss of traditional communication networks, social constraints were also lost.

Could there have been another way to save lives without destroying the unity of the Turkana people? It's always too easy to look back and say yes. Lifesaving change was needed, but without shattering foundations of the society. Change could have been introduced through the existing communication systems of the Turkana, rather than from outside. The people were attracted away from their long-standing social structures. Efforts could have been directed to maintain traditional communication networks and not simply to meet immediate physical needs. When the communication networks were broken, the social constraints were also broken and social degeneration began.

While the Turkana example shows the disintegration of an old, traditional society, it's also a picture of social disintegration that plagues the new, sprawling urban areas of the world. Disintegration isn't always a result of urbanization, but is common wherever familiar communication networks are shattered without replacement. New networks rapidly knit together a jumble of new people in new areas. Some of the networks are constructive, affirming values and practices that form a stable and productive community. Urban churches have often been the center of such networks when they deliberately seek to develop shalom[20] among their adherents, not limiting their ministry to worship services two or three times a week. It is tragic that counter-productive networks can also emerge rapidly, where anti-social behaviors ravage the stability of a community. Crime gangs form the dominant communication networks, complete with their special symbols in graffiti, clothing, and ritual initiations.

Genuine development will come when ideas for change are planted within the society, utilizing existing communication networks and stimulating formation of new and fruitful networks. Change comes from within as people discuss the possibilities and jointly decide what they can do and how they can do it best. The outsider is needed to give new ideas and show new possibilities, but only insiders can really "do" development! Development demands full understanding by the people. Understanding will come through discussions, questions, and the group decision's to try a new way. The only way this kind of participation can be gained is by using the existing communication networks.

Bruce Olson's work in South America among the Motilone illustrates change through use of existing communication networks. Olson didn't try to pull people away from their culture; rather he planted the message of Jesus Christ within their communication networks. He talked to his close friend Bobby, a Motilone who later became a leader among the people. This friend believed the message of Christ. At the appropriate time, Bobby told the rest of his tribe about Christ in a singing contest that was a highlight of the Motilone year. The people listened closely. Belief in Christ then spread rapidly through the tribe—their own communication methods had been used in their own channels to declare the new message.

Further change came in the same way. When medical help was needed, Olson instructed the herbalist (medicine man) in the use of antibiotics and other modern medicines. The herbalist used these medicines in the same situations where traditional medicines had been used. Little disruption in traditional ways resulted, but positive change occurred and health improved. Change was so rapid and successful that he was called to testify before government agencies and international aid programs.

Use of the existing communication networks demonstrates respect for the people and their culture. It more thoroughly penetrates the entire group with the change message, bringing more extensive discussion and deeper understanding. It's not only the most effective approach; it also most clearly demonstrates Christ's love for the people by not forcing them to become somebody else in order to develop.

Internal versus External Communication Systems

Two different communication approaches are used in cross-cultural communication: working through the *internal communication system* (ICS) and creating an *external communication system* (ECS).

The ICS is the system already present in a society. The society controls content and use. It includes the ways by which a society maintains its identity, shares information within the group, provides for participation of members in the society's concerns, and punishes unacceptable behavior. The forms of the ICS differ between groups.

In every case, the basic building block is the small interpersonal network including certain family members and close friends. This primary social network may develop through shared activities and interests, or because of blood relationship. It's in these small groups, normally from three to five people, that fullest discussion occurs and the basis of group decision is laid. Several interpersonal networks are included in larger, more formally structured meetings where decisions are reached.

Small interpersonal networks have favorite places for talking—in the fields, on hunts, in the market, in courtyards of houses, or on residential streets. Individuals are involved in more than one such network, so these groups link together communities and even larger groups. Through the interlinked networks, news spreads, new possibilities are shared, and almost all people take part in the decision-making process. This informal yet strong system is operated by the people themselves. Outsiders may plant new ideas or seek an opportunity to share new ways, but the people alone decide what to do about these new ways. They discuss and decide in the interpersonal networks; public meetings formalize the decisions.

The external communication system, on the other hand, isn't under the control of the people. The ECS doesn't "participate" in the key interpersonal networks, but is restricted to public means of communication. Outsiders determine what messages are given and in what form. The response expected is decided by the outsiders. Outsiders determine what's best for the people, allowing only limited opportunity for local people to express their opinion. Even when opinion is expressed, control remains in the hands of outsiders. In many parts of the world, the use of radio and television is an ECS. Schools and newspapers may all be part of the ECS.

Neither the form of the message nor the method used primarily determines whether a communication system is internal or external. It's rather a question of who has control over content and timing of messages. New methods such as the internet[21] may be introduced from outside, yet still quickly become part of the ICS. Using traditional forms doesn't ensure that internal communication occurs, if outsiders are controlling the content and timing of the message itself.

Oratory, for example, is usually an internal form of communication. Nevertheless, using oratory in church doesn't mean the church is part of the ICS. The people often listen as spectators, instead of asking their own questions and discussing the content presented. They have no control over what is said, but are observers watching outsiders talk and make decisions. Extensive spiritual change might well occur if the gospel were planted within the ICS, rather than using primarily external systems. As part of the ICS, the Christian message would be discussed everywhere in the basic interpersonal networks of society. At that level, decisions are developed and attitudes changed.

When outsiders try to help another group of people, external communication systems are often their primary tool. Literacy or language classes, schools, pictures, demonstrations, and sermons are common methods designed by outsiders. These methods are valuable; however, if they don't succeed in planting the content within the ICS, they will fail. To "improve" their effectiveness, better production techniques are learned. But control remains in the hands of outsiders who don't participate in the basic interpersonal networks. The methods and the message are still outside the society, and so regarded with indifference or ignored. Doing more of the same things will not change the response. "Shouting more loudly" may only increase resistance to the message.

Over time the external communication systems do bring about change, however. They're often efficient in reaching large numbers of people with information. Therefore, the ECS may begin to replace traditional meetings for sharing information. Strong interpersonal networks grow weaker, replaced by schools, churches, and development projects. The power for change steadily shifts from the insider to the outsider. Surely, some will think, that's an improvement in a society that has changed little over many centuries; surely it needs such outside help.

But the internal communication system also provided social controls and maintained group identity, as discussed earlier. When external systems replace the internal, social controls weaken and even disappear. The external communication system cannot fill this need, as is frequently evident in Western societies dominated by television and other impersonal mass media.[22] Along the way of change and development, people begin to get lost and society breaks apart. Even while the cash economy increases, signs of social decay begin to appear. The price of development seems very high. Must it always be that way?

When the ICS is consciously used, a different pattern develops. The existing communication networks are strengthened; along with that, social control is maintained. Change begins, largely under the control of the society itself. The people are able to maintain a respect for themselves and their culture.

Why then, doesn't all mission and development follow this pattern?

Working within the ICS means a slow beginning. Visible change doesn't appear as quickly, because time must be allowed for discussion in interpersonal networks. Information will be passed between friends instead of in public meetings. Time for questions and answers, for debate and objections is needed. When consensus must be gained before change begins, it seems there's no progress during the time of interpersonal discussions and evaluation. Change comes in tiny drops, one drop at a time. It also means that change comes by multiplication instead of addition. The drops come faster and faster, until change is like a flood.

In summary, two different communication systems or approaches are possible, internal and external. Using the internal system, a society can maintain its identity and cohesion. Change is under the control of the society itself, making it possible for development to begin without damaging the very group it seeks to help. An external communication system doesn't operate primarily within the forms and channels of the society; it's controlled from outside and consequently largely ignores felt needs of the group. It seeks to speak to the group rather than to individuals. There's limited opportunity for feedback, so the people have little opportunity to affect the message itself. An unintended consequence of the external system is the weakening of social control within the group.

Learning the Communication Networks

How is it possible to learn the communication networks in a society of which we're not a part? That takes longer than counting the number of houses in the village or the acreage given to different crops. Understanding the communication networks means understanding the people's way of life. Certain key things should be sought.

It's vital to *understand how close social relationships are maintained.* As an example, among the Lotuho, such relationships are maintained by sharing work and the giving of food and beer in exchange for work in the gardens. It's important to be hospitable and share your food with guests. Ritual and festive occasions such as times of thanksgiving, the Alam ceremonies (when God's blessing for the coming year is sought), marriages, and funerals—these maintain social relationships.

Among the Toposa, giving a bull to honor your friend is a very important way to maintain close relationship. The Chinese people exchange gifts of approximately equal value to maintain friendly relationships. And in America, visits to homes and going to special events together is used to maintain relationships.

Observe the society enough to know how those relationships are maintained, and you'll begin to observe the pattern of communication networks.

Learn how groups of people spend time together. What do they talk about? Is a decision reached or just information exchanged?

In rural America, the country trading store was a central point where people met, discussed happenings, and exchanged news. It was the key point in social networks. Among Kenya's Turkana, wedding feasts fulfill the same function. Since people come from dozens of miles around for the three or four days of feasting, news is exchanged, stories are told, and perhaps new marriages are arranged.

Social networks aren't often formally organized; it's the informal flow of information that's most influential. By observing and sharing in the discussion, the pattern can soon be understood. Only when the pattern of social communication is known and followed can an outside change agent begin to work effectively for change among that people.

Chapter Seventeen

Structure Affects Strategy

Communication is not merely with individuals, but with the society of which individuals are a part. It follows that the structure of the society must be understood before effective communication can be developed. We can't approach all societies in the same way because all societies aren't the same. A master plan that gives the same method for communicating with many different groups seldom succeeds because differences are overlooked—missing both unique opportunities and difficulties.

Freedom is a frequently expressed ideal in the West; everyone should be free to "do their own thing." Popular philosophy encourages people to do what feels good to them, and not to worry about the results for someone else. Every man is considered "an island," and responsibilities to others in the society are secondary. But such individualism is unreal, a product of imagination without substance. There must be concern for the whole society or the society will cease to exist! A collection of individuals does not make a society.

We're not concerned with judging a society or its ideals, simply understanding it. To understand a society and communicate with it, it's necessary to understand it as a whole. Society determines the effects of communication as much as, or more than, single individuals do. That's why knowing the relationships that bind people together in a functioning group (the structure of the society) is essential in achieving effective communication.

No society can be completely individualistic because individualism prevents any kind of structure, and without structure, individuals cannot achieve large purposes. We must accomplish large purposes to survive—to maintain security, provide for food, and how to interact with the environment. The strength of a society to accomplish large purposes is determined by the degree to which individuals can participate in and accept the authority of the overall structure.

As compared to other parts of the world, societies of South Sudan are relatively weak. A central authority larger than the tribe is only partially accepted. Family relationships are much stronger than relationships to a central governing authority. Each tribal group is too small by itself to withstand outside pressures. A consequence of this was the long practice of slaving in this region; the small groups were easy prey to larger, more powerfully organized outside groups.

This fundamentally affects development strategy. In some nations, development has occurred because of the interest and willingness of the central authority to create development. They give regulations and directives that are followed. The Asian societies that developed rapidly—Korea, Japan, Singapore, China—are societies that accepted strong central authority. The African societies, in general, are slow to accept a strong, central authority. Where they have in the past, great empires have arisen, such as Mali, Benin, and Ghana. More recently, the Zulus and Matabele of Southern Africa became great military powers because of strong central authority.

The myth of the all-powerful tribal chief who commands slavishly obedient subjects has blinded many to the real structure of African society. "If I can win the chief," the outsider thinks, "then I can reach my goal"—whether that goal is to start a church, launch economic development, or find gold. If "the chief" agrees, it's reported as a great victory. In practice, it may be important to gain the chief's consent, but he'll usually be unable to give it without the consent of his people. The structure of the society makes the chief accountable to the people, directly or indirectly. A similar relationship is noted between chief and people of North American Plains Indian tribes, and elsewhere among groups organized by clans or tribes.

For the purpose of understanding communication, we can identify three types of social structures, with many variations of each—*democratic, authoritarian,* and *consensus.*

Democratic Structure of Society

In a democratic society, rulers are accountable to the people they rule. Great diversity is possible within democratic societies. Various groups combine to gain power, at least for a time. New combinations of groups emerge, and these new groups gain power, if they persuade the majority that their interest will be served.

When considering how to create change and development in a democratic society, the determining factor is the accountability of the rulers to the majority of the people. Change must be seen to benefit the majority and must come from the people's desires rather than from government directives. If this doesn't happen, any government attempting unpopular change and development will soon be out of power. Program planning with the government leaders will not ensure success. The ultimate authorities—the people themselves—must be convinced through participation in decision-making.

Authoritarian Control of Society

The authoritarian government is not accountable to the people as a whole. There may be an accountability to controlling elites, the group that makes decisions for everybody and has control in many areas of life. An authoritarian government may use several kinds of power to enforce their decision and maintain control—physical, social, and mental. The majority of the population is forced to conform to central decisions and policies.

To create change in a country under authoritarian rule, the change-agent must begin with the authorities. If the authorities are convinced of the value of a development program, the door is opened to begin work with the people. The people are, of course, the true target for development efforts; the same process must be followed with the people as described earlier. Even after gaining government agreement or even sponsorship, it's necessary to gain the people's cooperation. Government decrees seldom create initiative in citizens, yet initiative is a key element in success.

There are many authoritarian governments in the world today, though not only governments operate in this manner. Business is often conducted in an authoritarian manner; the manager normally is not accountable to the employees but to the owners. Workers are told what they're to do, and what they must not do. Sometimes they may make suggestions, but the decision belongs to management, which is rarely accountable to the workers.

Education is often conducted in the same authoritarian fashion. The teacher's word is what counts, and the student must obey. In turn, the teacher must obey the headmaster's word, and the headmaster the board of governors. It's an authoritarian structure that seldom allows the students to question in any direct way.

The Consensus Society

In a consensus society, the leader expresses the desires and feelings of the group. To the outsider it appears that the leader is dictating to the group, but in actuality the leader normally expresses the group's decision achieved through group discussion. The leader cannot lead unless he has the support of the whole group. Consensus societies use much discussion, both in public meetings and private gatherings, during the decision process. Without thorough discussion, the consensus society would disintegrate into small groups, each with its own idea. Because consensus decision-making is based on ample discussion, these societies are usually small enough to be called face-to-face societies. Votes are seldom taken; the leaders sense when there's agreement on the matter being considered. At that point, the leader expresses the decision achieved in group process.

The leader of a consensus society is like the politician in a parade; as soon as he discovers in which direction the parade is going, he runs to the front to lead it. The leader doesn't so much determine the society's direction as express the direction the society is already going.

Individual opinions are rarely formed until the group as a whole forms an opinion. There are minor exceptions to this, of course, but seldom on major issues. If disagreement persists, talking will normally continue until the issue is resolved. This is difficult for Westerners to grasp, because education and tradition have made them individualistic. They've been trained to think independently, rather than to operate within a framework of consensus.

Consequently, when Westerners approach consensus societies (which are common in Africa, Asia, and Latin America), there's a tendency to search for a few key individuals and seek to influence them. It's assumed that they'll lead the rest of the society in making a desired decision. Often the strategy is to win the minds of the young, so they can win the society over to another point of view when they become older. Neither of these approaches is effective. Both assume that individuals make up their minds rather than recognizing that it's the society as a whole that decides.

The democratic process of decision-making seems slow when compared to the rapidity of the authoritarian process. The consensus process is the slowest of all. However it also develops the greatest degree of support from the people being governed. When a decision is made, the community has made the decision collectively, so they more fully support and implement the decision.

One-party government often develops in consensus societies that have adopted Western parliamentary practices. It's not necessarily an expression of authoritarian rule. Within the one party there's much discussion and room for differing approaches to decisions. But the discussions and decisions are internal. Decision is expressed publicly by the party leadership, then the party as a whole works to implement the decision. Two parties would be an invitation to disunity, since each party would be accountable to only part of the people.

A formal, public vote is often considered a dangerous step toward disunity. Unity is highly desired in a consensus society, and disagreements will be handled to reduce the possibility of serious disunity. A consensus society tries to keep all people equal and equally involved in the group. This extends to matters outside the normal concern of politics, including wealth or outstanding achievement. It's not considered wise or safe to be too much ahead of others in the group.

A friend from rural Zimbabwe had a brilliant son, who eagerly learned all he could before going elsewhere to get university work. I once asked the father, "What would have happened to your son if he had been born a hundred years ago?"

The father quickly responded that his son wouldn't have lived to become a man! His brilliance would have been seen as a threat to the group, rather than a help. One such man advancing far ahead of others in the group would have been considered a threat to group unity.

On another occasion I overheard two African builders repairing a foreigner's home in Zimbabwe. "Would you like to live in a nice house like this?" one asked.

"No," the second builder replied, "I wouldn't want to live in a house like this." There was a pause before he continued, "I wouldn't live very long if I had a nice house like this." He assumed that others would not let him be so far ahead of his group in having a fine house, so he would be "eliminated" to prevent him from becoming a source of disunity.

It's well to remember that this is the ideal held in a consensus society—that all share equally, and that no one advances too far ahead of others. Nevertheless the ideal isn't always kept. The real practice may be only a little different from the ideal, or very different.

In every life, there's a gap between the real that we practice and the ideal that we like to think we practice. The ideal will influence our acceptance of new ideas and new practices more than the real. We'll more readily accept the thing that helps us to achieve the ideal than something that denies or weakens the ideal.

The ideal is unity in a consensus society. In reality there will be some division. However, outsiders dare not introduce change in the society by exploiting those divisions, pitting one group against another. If their help is seen as a source of disunity and trouble, in due course it will be rejected by a group that has now united against them!

The ideal of unity in all things also hinders a few from becoming wealthy while most remain poor. Being the richest man doesn't necessarily give status. Status is gained by willingness to share the riches with other people. This is notably demonstrated among the First Nations of Canada, such as the Haida, Kwakiutl, and Tlingit. Consequently, it isn't possible to accumulate wealth and still be an accepted part of their society. Accumulation of wealth without sharing is considered anti-social, a threat to the community, and a cause of disunity. Such a person will often be ignored by the community or forced to leave.

The obligations of the extended family often prevent much accumulation of wealth by an individual. The wealthy man typically has obligations that increase as his wealth increases. Thus, the accumulation of capital for investment and development is virtually impossible in traditional consensus societies.

In urbanizing areas throughout the world, these attitudes to wealth accumulation are changing, often causing confusion and divisions within formerly unified groups. A byproduct of the shift from subsistence farming to a cash economy is the growth of individualism. Urbanization almost always means the breakdown of a consensus society. It's economically impossible to operate in a traditional fashion within an urban setting. In the country, when more people come, they help grow more crops so there will be enough for all. In the city, you can't grow more money when more people move in with you. Nevertheless, the ideal of a unified society is still strong, even in the midst of these significant changes.

As a way to start development, giving a few individuals special opportunities is usually unwise. Demonstrating through them the superiority of new methods may result in those individuals being rejected by their society. Their success at a time when others in the society are failing may create resentment and opposition, instead of encouraging imitation.

If individuals try different methods, following full discussion with the group, they may indeed demonstrate the way to development for the group. The key is in maintaining participation in the group, not doing new things apart from group awareness and tacit agreement that it can be tried. The group knows that if the new approach doesn't work, they bear responsibility to help and to keep the innovative man from starving. So group awareness of trial change is an understandable protection for the group.

In working with another society, we must approach it on the basis of that society's structure and patterns, not on those of our own society. Just as water is shaped by the container holding it, so our communication must be shaped by the society within which we're seeking to stimulate development.

PART SIX

Does Change Mean Progress?

Every culture is constantly changing. The environment, neighboring groups, governments, size of populations, available resources—nothing stays constant. The society must adjust to those changes or disappear, at best absorbed by a more adaptable group. At the worst, it will be destroyed.

The issue is not whether a culture will change, but what it will become when it does change. The society must be cautious and conservative, responding to change in a way that will most benefit itself. Trusting their survival to an outsider seems too great a risk.

The effective change agent will accept this necessary caution, making haste slowly for the long-term benefit of the people.

Chapter Eighteen

Deciding to Change

Change is something like the germination of seeds. What happens beneath the surface of the ground, out of sight, determines if the seed will grow. We see only the tip of the new plant breaking through the surface of the ground, and we say the seed has germinated. That's neither the beginning nor the end of our concern for the seed. We must protect it until it is strong; we must provide food for the plant and keep weeds from growing up and crowding it. At the right season, the seed will give us the flower or the fruit we want.

At what point could we say that the seed is grown? At no single point, because growth is something that starts when the seed is buried in the earth, continuing until it produces the desired crop. At different steps, different needs of the plant had to be met.

It's the same with the growth of a child. The baby is born after a nine-month pregnancy, but when did the baby's life begin? Life begins before the baby is born, and after the birth a great deal of care is needed to help the child grow to maturity.

In a similar way, change doesn't happen when a decision is made publicly. It began long before a public choice was made, involving at least six recognizable stages before and after a public decision. The process of change is best seen as a circular movement; one step toward change leads to another, usually without any sharply defined beginning point. Change is a continuous process growing out of discontent with the present and awareness of alternative possibilities.

Awareness

The first step toward change is awareness that an alternative is available. Until someone knows another way exists, they cannot follow that other way! For centuries, millions have lived in deep poverty, plagued by famine and disease. There was little dissatisfaction among these millions of people because they didn't know of any alternative. Then with the arrival of early travelers (considered "explorers" by Europeans), other alternatives began to be seen. Missionaries came intent on showing God's love by overcoming disease and improving the people's way of life. Finally, tourists came displaying wealth that poverty-bound people had never imagined. With the entrance of radios, books, and magazines, and then motion pictures and television, most of these billions saw that there was another possibility. They didn't have to live in the hopelessness of sickness and starvation.

Interest

Social scientists referred to this result as "the rising aspirations of the multitudes." With first contact, the people weren't interested in any alternative because it seemed a possibility only for others. With increasing exposure, a few, then many, began to think, "Perhaps there's something better for me." Interest in the alternatives caused the "problem" of rising aspirations.

Evaluation

Friends discuss these possibilities. They speculate why some people have so much more than they do. They consider whether they could make changes to bring some of these benefits to themselves. Often in these conversations there's inadequate information, so explanations are often deficient;

there's no way for the friends to know their information is incomplete and often inaccurate. Consideration is given to what is possible, and what it would cost socially or in terms of their wealth to do things in a different way. Outside experts are of little value at this stage, because evaluation is done in interpersonal networks, the basic units of any society.

Choice

Following evaluation, a choice is made. Evaluation may convince them that the new way would be better, or that it's too full of risk and might destroy more than it helps. This choice is private, often made in intimate small groups, families, or with close friends.

Attempts from the outside to persuade a person or group have little effect. Many people respond to such persuasive efforts by stubbornness—they become more convinced of their *existing* choice or attitude. Most, however (around 75 percent) simply ignore the persuasive effort. A few do change in the desired way (about 5 percent), but an equal number change in the opposite way! The effort to persuade them is seen as manipulation of their choice; resentment results in a negative view of the persuasive effort.

When new information is given while people are considering their choice, the decision process reverts to the evaluation stage, necessary to incorporate the new information in the process.

Implementation

Very soon after the choice there must be an opportunity for implementation of that choice. If the choice is made to try a new variety of seed, for example, the farmer must be able to actually acquire and plant the seed. If he cannot do this because supplies aren't available, he's unable to follow through with the choice he has made. It's as though he never made the choice.

Opportunity must be given for public expression in words or actions, or the choice will not be acted upon. If it isn't acted upon, it's lost. Once lost in this way, it's difficult to again bring the person to the point of choice. A resistance may develop because it's thought, "I tried that once and I couldn't make it work." A degree of immunity to that change is the result.

Nothing is achieved if, after people are persuaded to make a choice for change, the change is impossible to implement. To persuade people to have clean drinking water when they have no borehole, no way to filter the water, or not enough wood to boil the water, is worse than pointless. Failing to make implementation easy simply increases resistance to any other changes that are proposed.

Readjustment

Implementation always leads to readjustment. Every change creates other changes. A simple choice to change the variety of seed used is implemented by obtaining new seed from a cooperative, a merchant, or agricultural demonstrators. The change can be implemented, but at least one necessary readjustment is present. In the past, seed came from the crop of the year before and was raised by the farmer himself. It was stored in his storehouses for the next year's planting. Now the farmer must go to someone else for that seed. That involves travel, along with developing a trust in someone else who may be outside his own clan or tribe. It also involves payment. How can he buy the seed, or what can he exchange for the seed? Several new elements enter into his life. Readjustment is necessary.

A husband may be convinced that boiled water is necessary for drinking, and he demands it from his wife. That means readjustment for her—finding more wood to keep the fire going longer to boil water, having another pot in which the water is boiled and stored. The husband may be convinced of the value of these readjustments, but he doesn't do the work. Is the wife convinced? The possible readjustments caused by even the simplest change in a society seem endless. It's like throwing a stone into a still pool of water; the ripples spread further and further. As other stones are tossed in, the pool's stability is shattered and everything is in upheaval. Probable readjustments must be considered before change is introduced to a group.

Change is a continuous process; one stage leads directly into the next. No sharp steps are visible. Change may stop, and resistance to further change develop, if each part cannot progress.

All problems cannot be recognized in advance, of course. Outsiders may not even be aware of problems when they arise during change. Therefore it's necessary that the change be implemented *with* the community, through continuing involvement between the change agent and those who are attempting to change.

A simple example illustrates how easy it is for change agents to misunderstand resistance. An aid agency decided it was important that all employees begin work promptly in the morning. Tardiness was penalized by some loss of salary. Despite the penalty and repeated warnings, one employee continued to begin work late most mornings. When he was called in for a final warning before dismissal, the supervisor discovered that the man was very willing to come on time, but he didn't know what time it was—he had no clock.

How can communication be useful in starting the process of change?

Communication functions both *publicly* and *interpersonally*. Public communication involves media such as radio and television, through which the message is given with little or no face-to-face contact. Drama may be utilized, or pictures, demonstrations, and speeches, all of which give limited opportunity for interaction between people. Interpersonal communication (which could also be called private media) is one-to-one, or within a small group, in conversations or through social media. It involves heavy interaction in small groups.

Both public and private media are important in the process of change, but in different ways.

In the stages of awareness and interest, public media is most important. Communication tools like radio, newspapers, and public discussions can make people aware of the possibility of change. Drama, speeches, and teaching in the schools let people know that alternatives to present ways exist.

In contrast, evaluation of these suggestions and the choice to try them will primarily come in small group discussion in the family and between friends. These interpersonal networks are the basic building block of any society. It's there that new ideas will be considered, then chosen or rejected. If public media hasn't done a good job of giving all necessary information, these interpersonal networks cannot function well, and wrong choices—or no choices—will be made. If the public media try to force a choice before there has been time to evaluate and make a choice privately, rejection is also likely.

In the stages of implementation and readjustment, both public media and inter-personal networks are used. Ways to implement change, and help to make the necessary readjustments, can be learned through the public media. However, it's with the help of family and friends that necessary modifications will be made and courage gained to continue on a path of change.

It's clear that there must be careful use of the public media so that they feed into interpersonal networks. Their critical role should not be overlooked. It isn't a question of which is best, but rather which is the most appropriate at each stage of change.

Points to Remember

When we introduce economic or religious changes, this model of decision-making suggests certain important points to be observed, summarized below.

1. We must realize the importance of interpersonal networks, rather than depending only on visible public media. More change may result from a shared cup of tea than from hours of public speeches.

2. Specialists cannot create change by themselves. Unless the people are also involved, the message will simply not be considered in the interpersonal networks. In matters of belief and faith, the layman is often a more effective evangelist than the professional pastor.

3. The use of public media must be related to interpersonal networks in order to be effective. Public media by itself may be highly visible yet ineffective in producing change.

4. Public media should seldom urge an immediate choice, but should encourage discussion within interpersonal networks where the decision normally occurs.

5. Opportunities for a public statement of choice must be given to reinforce private decisions. This principle is stated clearly in Romans 10:9-10: "If you will confess with your mouth Jesus as Lord, and believe in your heart that God raised him from the dead, you will be saved. For with the heart you believe and receive righteousness, and with the mouth you confess and are saved." Inward belief is incomplete without outward commitment. In this regard, change in culture is similar to spiritual change.

6. Interpersonal relationships must be established with (and between) people who make a commitment to change. Build networks of people who have made a decision to

change in any area. Mutual support and counsel are an essential part of the change process.

Change is much more than a decision. It's a process that begins almost invisibly, ultimately affecting parts of life far beyond the initial area of change. Understanding what's involved will help us to be better prepared at each point to help those involved in major change.

Chapter Nineteen

Change Without Tragedy

It may be called development, modernization, evangelism, or church-planting. All these efforts are attempts to change part or all of another culture. There are good reasons to introduce change—so that people will produce more food, or be freed from constant disease, or be brought to fullness of life through Jesus Christ. All are desirable. But sharing these benefits always involves changing the culture of the receivers in some way.

What's involved in changing cultures?

The thirteen principles listed below provide reminders of the most desirable ways to create change, and they alert the cross-cultural worker to danger areas. All these principles assume that change is deliberately introduced from outside by a group committed to create change—social, physical, economic, or spiritual. Such groups may be development agencies, government agencies, educational programs, or churches.

The principles can be examined in four categories.

Introduction of Change

The first set of principles looks at how proposed changes or innovations are introduced.

1. While introducing change, strengthen group respect for its own traditions, and the group's appreciation of itself.

The obvious purpose for bringing change is to increase the group's welfare. Though concentrating on changes, the emotional welfare of the group must be remembered. That can be maintained and even improved by increasing the society's respect for its own history, traditions, and valuable culture patterns even while change is introduced.

Never should the people be made to feel that their culture is worthless, bad, or unimportant. Belittling people destroys their self-respect slowly and surely, opening the way to serious social breakdown.

2. An innovation will be accepted if: a) it meets a felt need in the society; and b) it fits with existing cultural patterns.

Earlier, we discussed the value of felt needs as a beginning point in introducing change. Every society has needs that occupy its attention. The needs may be fundamental, like food and health, or they may be for relaxation and finding self-fulfillment. Regardless of the kind of need, no innovation will be accepted if it isn't seen to meet felt needs.

Offering to build new school buildings and train more teachers is a long-range contribution toward improving living standards. If people are in the midst of a severe famine or being plundered by a dominant group, their immediate felt need is not for education but for food and protection. Even if education would be valuable, immediate plans must center on meeting the needs that dominate people's minds.

Further, the innovation must be something that fits with existing cultural patterns. For example, if it requires people to learn completely new ways of doing a familiar activity, or creates a major shift in the roles of men and women, it isn't likely that the innovation will be accepted even if it would meet a major felt need.

Cultural patterns are familiar and comfortable. They provide a sense of ease and emotional security. Abrupt change in culture patterns is disturbing at the least. In some cases it causes emotional damage and mental illness, and disintegration of families and communities. Rather than risk the uncertainty of changing cultural patterns, most people refuse the innovation.

3. Change should be introduced through the communication systems controlled by the society itself.

Modern communication methods are powerful and efficient in reaching many people quickly. Almost always, however, they're under the control of an outside group instead of the group that's being changed. These outside communication methods compete with the methods already used within the society, often replacing the traditional methods. At first glance, that seems simply a matter of using a better way. But as we discussed earlier, social controls are destroyed when the indigenous communication system is weakened or discarded.

It's the communication system that gives the group its sense of unity and identity. If communication is controlled by people outside the group, quite obviously there will be no way for the group to maintain an internal sense of oneness. Without communication, a group will break apart leaving its members with a sense of aloneness. Change introduced through the internal communication systems avoids destroying the group in the process of improving its way of life.

4. The value of an innovation is determined by those who are to use it, not by those who offer it.

It's an easy thing to stand apart from the difficulties of someone else's life and make suggestions about how they could do things better. But for whom is the proposed innovation most important? The person who thought of it, or the person who actually puts it into use? No matter how splendid the idea may seem, only the person who tries it can say whether it's valuable.

Development schemes, five-year plans, church-planting strategies, and self-help programs do not meet their real test of worth in councils, boards, or parliaments. Their real test is in the communities where people decide whether they'll follow the proposed innovations. Discuss new ideas with the people, and make plans with them—they're the ones who'll decide the success or failure of the innovations.

5. Change is easy if fundamental cultural values aren't affected; change is difficult when those values are questioned or contradicted.

It's not a major cultural change to introduce the innovation of guns in a fighting society where raiding with spears or bows and arrows is common. The fundamental attitude of fighting isn't changed or challenged. The change only gives a "better way" to fight. That's not a deep change, but one that fits existing cultural values. Trying to stop all raiding between tribes, however, would call for fundamental change in values and practice. People who have lived for generations with the pride and fear of raiding will usually reject attempts to stop it.

Any change that contradicts core values will be rejected. Arguments, education, demonstrations—none of them will change people if they see a possibility of losing something basic in their culture.

The central value of many semi-nomadic people (such as the Bedouin or Toposa) is livestock, frequently valued more highly than the lives of children and women when survival is a question. When there's a short water supply, men dig deep holes in sandy river beds to get enough water to keep the cattle alive. Laboriously, as water seeps into the bottom of the sandy well, it's scooped up and lifted into hollowed-out log troughs where the cattle wait to drink. No such effort is made to get water for the women and children. They may use the holes after the cattle are finished, but most often they must look elsewhere.

The innovation of wells and pumps is quickly accepted—when cattle are allowed around the well. But if fences are put up to keep the well area clean, the fencing will be destroyed. In some cases, the entire innovation of wells and pumps is rejected if cattle aren't permitted around the well.

An acceptable innovation will harmonize with the fundamental values of the people. When those values are ignored, the innovation is modified or rejected. By introducing wells in a way consistent with existing values, the cattle, as well as the women and children, will be helped. When outsiders impose their standards on use and maintenance of the well, the whole project is jeopardized.

Change Agents

The second set of principles involve the role of change agents.

6. *Use people who have prestige in their own society to introduce change.*

Decisions are normally made after much group discussion. Nevertheless, someone must be the first to introduce the subject and begin the discussion. For the best possible consideration of an innovation, the person who carries the suggestion to the group should be respected by the group. That person should be active in the group, both on formal occasions and during the informal social times that bond a group together.

A person without prestige in the group may sometimes seem, however, to be a good individual to introduce an innovation. Well-educated, holding an important government position, and progressive in personal practices, all are valuable qualifications to be a change agent. But if the group itself doesn't consider that person to be part of their social networks, the innovation will probably be ignored. Perhaps at a later time the suggestion will be remembered. It might then be discussed, after they've forgotten who originally introduced the idea. Most often, however, the innovation is never tried. It's simply forgotten because the one introducing it had not earned a hearing within the society.

7. Leadership for change must come from within the society.

Suggestions for change in a society often come from outside the group. New ways of solving a common problem are seen elsewhere by travelers. These new solutions are "borrowed," and with some modification, introduced at home.

Change also comes from deliberate introduction of new ways by development agencies and missions. A need is seen and the outsiders make suggestions for meeting that need. Because they've drawn from experience in many places, these outside groups are well equipped to bring ideas for change. They can also provide demonstration and instruction in the new method. The people themselves, however, observe the change and adapt it to meet their own needs. They're aware of their cultural values and patterns, their own felt needs, and their abilities. They also know their environment and available resources. They're best equipped to shape innovations to suit their own culture. If outsiders don't encourage people to take the idea and shape it for themselves, many helpful changes will never be tried. Outside leadership cannot give the inside leadership essential for constructive change.

Group Interaction

Basic guides for interaction between groups involved in culture change are given in the third set of principles.

8. Make communication easy between the groups involved in change.

Planned development work always has at least two groups of people—the group to be helped and the group helping. They may be called the insiders and the outsiders, or nationals and expatriates. Each group has its own way of living and doing business. Each moves in its own circle and follows its own way of life, and only on planned occasions will have contact with the other group. These occasions of contact are reported back to the home circle and discussed widely. In talking, the facts often become changed and distorted. Suspicion begins to build, not because of bad motives but because of incomplete understanding. Neither group has enough opportunity to talk with the other to build better understanding.

Easy flow of communication between these two groups must be made possible. Good communication will reduce the possibility of rejection and conflict. With good communication, success is probable; without it, failure will be the result of even the most excellent programs.

9. There must be mediators between the groups involved in change.

Development and mission work is deliberate change. A program is introduced that will change ways of living. And the inside group already has a plan for living that has enabled them to survive. If it didn't work, they would be dead! One group is trying to change another group. Misunderstanding is very likely. These different groups come from different places, have different cultures, speak different languages, and have different beliefs about the nature of the world. To expect them to understand each other easily is unrealistic. How do you handle the misunderstandings?

Mediators are needed, people who have the confidence of both groups. Some of these mediators will come from among the insiders and some from the outsiders. Some will be educated; others will have never been to school. The important quality of mediators is the trust of people in both groups. They can speak to both groups and be sure that people will listen. Even if a mediator is from the inside group, he understands enough about the outside point of view and goals so that he can explain those clearly to others in his group. He'll also have the ability to explain his group's beliefs and desires to the outside group.

Mediators will usually be part of a "third culture," as spoken of in Chapter 11. In the third culture, people from different cultures begin to understand each other and are then ready to explain outsider and insider viewpoints. Understanding is essential for successful efforts to stimulate development. Good, necessary work will be destroyed by distrust, arguments, and accusations. Mediators provide the necessary channel to smooth the way for change.

Group Response

In the final set of principles, the response of the receiving group is considered.

10. Change in one part of a society will bring change throughout the whole society.

Societies are social systems that give some security to members, helping to solve the problems of survival. Like any system, every part depends upon every other part. If one part is taken away, change is forced throughout the whole system in order to make up for the loss.

A society could be compared to an automobile (though a society is far more complex than that). When the car is running smoothly, we don't think about each individual part, commenting on how well the crankshaft turns, or how rapidly the radiator is cooling the engine. But if a small hole is put in the radiator, so that it can no longer hold water, soon the whole engine will become overheated and stop. Merely one small hole in the wrong place can stop the whole car.

Just so, changing the ways of food production can change the relationships between men and women and also create pressure to find new ways to store excess grain. By providing more reliable food supplies the number of children who grow into adults will increase. That brings increasing population and thus pressures for more land.

Changing any part of the culture may cause disaster when launched by inexperienced or thoughtless people. The possible consequences of change proposals must be considered before introducing change.

11. Don't take something away without giving something back.

There are times when a cultural practice must be stopped because it's preventing the people from adopting a better way. In every culture there are traditional practices that may destroy good health or violate God's ways for good living. However, such practices should not be stopped until a substitute is introduced. This substitute should fulfill the same function in the society as the original practice. This functional equivalent reduces the possibility of social disorganization and hostile reactions to the changes being introduced.

In Kenya, for example, charcoal-making is leading to the cutting of many trees. Forested areas are being destroyed and desert is creeping into formerly productive agricultural areas. Laws have been made prohibiting cutting of trees in some areas and requiring permits in others. But cutting continues because charcoal is the only available cooking fuel for poorer people in the cities. The cities continue to grow, demand for charcoal rises, and the desert advances as trees are cut down. Until a functional equivalent for charcoal is introduced, no law or police force can stop the desertification of Kenya.

In Burundi, excessive drinking of banana beer has caused widespread problems—drunkenness, quarrels, and wasteful use of limited food resources. Beer also has an old and strongly established place in the culture as a way by which all kinds of social contracts are sealed, to give refreshment for those working on their neighbors' lands, and as an integral part of social conversation. But because of the problems of excessive drinking, missionaries forbade the use of beer to Christian converts. The ban on beer caused many people to leave their Christian commitment, and caused much misunderstanding between missionaries and the Burundi people.

What other solution could there be to the problem? Drunkenness is destructive both individually and to the whole society. Of course, if there's no beer, no one will fall into drunkenness. Even so, beer is necessary for social arrangements, for conversation, and even for payment of labor. Is there something else that would fill the same functions?

After considering this, some church groups tried the introduction of coffee, also grown in Burundi. Others began to use soft drinks. The use of some functional equivalent reduced the resentment and resistance that came with a total ban.

In Nigeria, one tribe held an annual ceremony at which all brides of that year were blessed by the river god. Christian pastors from that tribe were troubled because even those who were Christians sought the river god's blessing in violation of God's commandment not to have any other gods before Him. Without the river god's blessing, it was thought there would be no children in the marriage. Nobody was willing to risk such consequences.

Then the pastors decided to hold a blessing ceremony for new brides in the church on the very same day that the river god ceremony was conducted. Christian brides were encouraged to take part in it instead of the traditional river god ritual. Some tried this functional equivalent. There was great rejoicing in the church when within the next year, every one of the brides who had been in the church ceremony had a baby.

Forbidding a practice by teaching or by force will seldom eliminate the practice. Introducing a functional equivalent provides a substitute so that the society isn't disrupted. It can be compared to removing a pillar holding up a roof. The pillar may be rotting and in need of replacement. But before the old pillar is pulled down, a new one must be put into place.

12. A group may passively accept changes forced by outside pressure, but at the same time, develop strong reactions that suddenly erupt in violence.

Outside pressures to change may overwhelm a group. They feel there's no choice but to accept the change and bend to the pressure. They may outwardly continue to be passive and accepting, while inward resentment is increasing. Their sense of security is threatened by forced loss of familiar ways. Even where physical security may be increased, emotional security is seriously damaged.

Then one or two people begin to talk about their objections. Such talk spreads to a small group. Several small groups then discuss it quietly, and it filters throughout a much larger group. As pressure increases, bitterness grows. Talking spreads that bitterness. At some point, the group can no longer stand the tension and explosion occurs. The explosion is often caused by something that appears to have no relationship to the source of pressure—the death of a prized animal, the arrest of someone caught in theft, the discharge of a man from his job, a shopkeeper defrauding a customer, or even a natural disaster such as a sudden storm.

It's somewhat like the bursting of a balloon. The hole made in the balloon is very tiny, but the air rushes out and tears the balloon apart with a great bang. It's impossible to return the balloon to wholeness again. Similarly, a social explosion causes so much damage that the society cannot go back to what it was before.

What kind of pressures lead to these tragic explosions?

One source is the strict enforcing of a law that seems unjust or that denies traditional rights. In South Africa, the pressures built up among the Black African population who were continually troubled by the system of apartheid, though seemingly accepting what was happening. When new legislation was introduced that would have denied use of English in their education, a series of riots tore through the African areas of Johannesburg. The language issue by itself did not cause the rioting; it was simply the prick that burst the balloon.

In China, foreign powers carved out areas of influence, demanding special rights for missionaries and merchants. Chinese rights were not protected, Chinese culture was belittled, and a proud people were forced to serve the interests of foreigners whom they disliked and didn't trust. The explosion came through a secret society called the Boxers, which led to a rebellion that swept through China, killing hundreds. Nobody was prepared for the rebellion except the rebels.

Any society under heavy outside pressure will develop some resistance. To avoid a destructive reaction, every possible means should be used to reduce pressure on a culture undergoing change.

13. During periods of rapid change, indicators of social difficulties must be carefully watched.

Four useful indicators of social difficulties will point to a troubled society in which potentially explosive reactions are building: 1) change in moral standards; 2) increase in factionalism; 3) migration; and 4) increase in personal tension and anxiety.

When moral standards change sharply from what they traditionally have been, this shows that family relationships are troubled. A rising number of illegitimate births, increase of theft, more drunkenness especially among the younger people, and an increase in violent crimes all reveal spreading social decay. Declining moral standards are a clear symptom of a people under pressure.

Examples of this are evident in most major urban areas of the world. In Johannesburg, more than half of all births are reported to be illegitimate. The frequency of violent robbery in Nairobi has created a large security guard business protecting private homes. Parts of New York City, Chicago, Lagos, and other major urban centers of the world are unsafe for the casual visitor. Alcoholism in the United States, Russia, and France (to name only three of the troubled nations) is called a growing epidemic. The change in moral standards isn't limited to urban areas; it's just more easily seen where many people are crowded together.

The second indicator, factionalism, is the breaking down of a large group into smaller groups that begin to quarrel. The issues may be political, economic, or religious. It doesn't matter whether the outside pressure comes from a development agency, a church, the government, or enemy raiders. When the pressure is more than can be easily handled, a society begins to break into smaller and smaller groups.

A persistent quarrel among Sudan's Lotuho as to which rainmaker should be followed is an example of rising factionalism. Instead of a single tribe with four or five major divisions into "rain areas," divisions increased. Where formerly one area followed one rainmaker, two or three groups each followed a different aspiring rainmaker. Instead of four or five subdivisions, seven or more now function. This is one indication of reaction against strong pressures to change.

When factionalism becomes extreme, groups of people simply move away from those who have become their enemies. When individuals or groups can no longer handle the pressure, migration to a new territory, to cities, or to another nation becomes frequent. Madi from Uganda fled into Sudan; educated Ugandans took refuge in Kenya, Britain, and the United States. All were escaping the pressures of various regimes in Uganda.

Tens of thousands of Mexicans enter the United States as illegal immigrants. Pakistanis find ways into Britain, and Turks stay in West Germany even when dismissed from their jobs. Economic pressures in their homeland stimulate migration to find better opportunities.

At the individual level, there's almost always a rise in tension and anxiety when change is too rapid. Stress is shown by anger, fighting, quarreling, and bitterness. Families are divided by increasing violence in the home. Bitterness between former friends damages personal relationships. Mutual help in work and overcoming personal difficulties is less common. Celebrations and ceremonies that have traditionally been peaceful are spoiled more frequently by anger and even fighting.

The mission, development, or government agency that doesn't carefully watch these indicators may have a tragic surprise in its future.

Chapter Twenty

Change Equals Risk

Change is dangerous, so why not leave people as they are?

It's a myth to think that change doesn't happen until missionaries or development workers enter people's lives. Change is already happening, even without the special objectives of change agents. The important question is, What kind of change?

People borrow technology and ideas, then adapt those to their own situation. They create new answers to continuing problems.

Societies aren't like immovable granite mountains, but more like a flowing river. The river follows nearly the same course year after year, but adapts to the change of seasons, the changes of vegetation on its banks, and changing rainfall. Cultures adapt to changing demands seeking the best way to ensure security and survival. The patterns of culture are constantly shifting as a result, yet the overall flow of the culture remains much the same.

Changing a river may seem desirable, placing a dam so that fields can be irrigated or floods can be kept safely within the river banks. Engineers try to carefully consider all the results of the change, making plans to prevent destructive damage. Sometimes a single "good" change brings consequences that are damaging in other areas. Good engineering and good policy-making stops the development at that point. The loss would be greater than the gain.

With the entry of outsiders who deliberately seek to introduce change, new possibilities and new dangers arise. Long-term as well as short-term results must be considered. Attempts to predict unintended consequences are necessary to avoid damage where help is intended. The challenge to stimulate change that improves a people's way of life demands both technical and social skills.

Most of all, seeking to help other people demands caring for other people. They cannot be viewed primarily as sick bodies, hungry children, or inefficient farmers. They're more than potential converts to Christianity. They're individuals whom God made to have dominion over His creation. Instead, the creation has dominion over them. They live, and die, dependent on forces which they can neither moderate nor control. This is surely not what God desires.

So we enter into lives with the purpose of helping them become all that God desires them to be. That must include spiritual reconciliation with God, physical care, and social strengthening to make whole people.

Through wholeness of mission, we'll have the reward of seeing the world's neglected fill the role for which God made them.

A Communication Framework

The propositions below provide a framework for effective utilization of communication. Twenty-three were presented originally in *Creating Understanding*[23] and are here revised to eighteen. None are omitted, but some are combined to avoid redundancy and increase ease of memory and use. Two have been added to highlight the essential spiritual dimension. The numbers in brackets indicate the numbering in *Creating Understanding*, 1992.

Propositions of Integrated Christian Communication

1. Communication is involvement. [1]
2. Communication is a process. [2]
3. Communication is what is heard, not only what is said. [3]
   - 3.1. Meaning is perceived internally and individually. [4]
4. Spiritual perception and response is the work of God's Spirit.
5. Mastery of content is the necessary foundation for effective communication. [6]
6. Clarification of goals increases the possibility of effective communication. [5]
7. The communicator's personality and experiences modify the form of the message. [7]

8. The communicator's image of the audience and understanding of the context are primary factors in shaping the form of the message. [8]

   8.1. A communicator almost always communicates with multiple audiences. [9]

9. Perceived and actual feedback shapes the form of the message. [23]

10. Communication increases commitment. [10]

11. All human communication occurs through the use of twelve signal systems. [11, 12]

    11.1. Usage of the signal systems is a function of culture; thus they're used differently in different cultures.

12. Mass media extend the range of a message and inevitably change the message. [13]

13. The effectiveness of a medium is largely determined by factors other than the medium itself. [15]

    13.1. Effectiveness normally decreases with increasing size of the audience. [14]

14. The cultural patterns and beliefs of a society fundamentally influence the form of effective communication. [17, 18]

15. Perception precedes comprehension, interpretation, and effect of a message. All are directly related to experience and needs. [19]

16. There are three simultaneous dimensions in communication process and effect—relational, emotional, and spiritual. [20]

17. People respond to communication as members of social groups. [21]

    17.1. Messages are mediated. [16]

18. A decision to change results from the combined effects of public [mass] media and interpersonal network. [22]

§

Notes

[1] Information as used here has a precise technical meaning referring to the amount of **information** given as measured in "bits"—binary information units. In communication theory it is a quantitative measure.

[2] WACC Bulletin—find bibliographic reference.

[3] Keller's best-selling *The Reason for God* (New York: Riverhead Books, 2009) is a fine linear development of Christian truth, appropriately aimed at the twenty-first-century New Yorker. "What is not traditional is Dr. Keller's skill in speaking the language of his urbane audience" (*New York Times*).

[4] Marshall McLuhan has expanded this perspective in *The Gutenberg Galaxy* (Toronto: University of Toronto Press, 1966) and *The Medium Is the Massage* (New York: Random House, 1967).

[5] *Rappings*, compiled by Robert Webber (Wheaton, Illinois: Tyndale House, 1971).

[6] *Lutheran World Information* (Geneva: 1982).

[7] Bruce Olson, *Bruchko* (Lake Mary, Florida: Charisma House, 2006; first published 1973).

[8] Suggestions for increasing effectiveness of your cross-cultural involvement are given in Chapter 13, "Using a Third Culture."

[9] The twelve different languages of culture are introduced in Chapters 10 and 11.

[10] John Koessler, "Worship of The Trajectory," *Christianity Today* (vol. 55, no. 3, March 2011).

[11] Carolyn Butler, "There's a Biological Basis to Feelin' Groovy," Portland *Oregonian* (March 10, 2011).

[12] William Barclay, *The Gospel of John,* vol. 2, revised ed. (Philadelphia: Westminster John Knox, 1975), 47.

[13] Lacking understanding of the values of the economy of affection expressed in the potlatch, both government and church authorities sought to make the practice illegal. The suppression was largely unsuccessful.

[14] Excellent explanation and helpful guides to understanding and using Hofstede's work are available at www.geerthofstede.nl/culture/dimensions-of-national-cultures.aspx — and www.clearlycultural.com/geert-hofstede-cultural-dimensions/.

[15] It is the work of philosophers to attempt identification and clarification of these assumptions. Frequently, the assumptions identified are considered universal, rather than as true only for their own culture. Each philosophy essentially expresses the assumptions of the philosopher's culture, building their framework of thought from that point.

[16] Various terms are used for the nations and peoples that are not part of the economic and political powers that dominate the world—Third World, Global South, and Majority World are the most common in the early twenty-first century.

[17] How do we learn the core beliefs? The formal ideology is far less important in a culture than the largely hidden informal beliefs that primarily determine perception and resulting actions, as noted above. In this introduction to effective intercultural communication, we can point out the need to learn but cannot teach how to learn these beliefs. A guide for learning in the field is a separate subject.

[18] Susan Olasky, *World* (vol. 26, no. 5, March 12, 2011).

[19] Scattering of soil over a group is a call for group participation among the Lotuho people in South Sudan.

[20] *Shalom* is Hebrew, expressing the wholeness of God's peace in every area of life.

[21] Social media forms such as Facebook, Twitter, LinkedIn, etc. are part of the internal communication system of a society. They're clearly controlled by users, often defying the efforts at control by governments and non-local forces. This was clearly shown in the rebellions throughout the Middle East in 2011, fueled almost entirely through social media.

[22] Marshall McLuhan has provocatively explored the impact of mass media in his writings such as *The Medium Is the Massage, The Gutenberg Galaxy,* and *Understanding Media: The Extensions of Man.*

[23] Donald K. Smith, *Creating Understanding: A Handbook for Christian Communication Across Cultural Landscapes* (Grand Rapids, Michigan: Zondervan, 1992).

§

Bibliography

Barclay, William. The Gospel of John, vol. 2, revised edition. Philadelphia, PA: Westminister Press, 1975.

Butler, Carolyn. "There's a Biological Basis to Feelin' Groovy." Portland, Oregon: The Oregonian, March 10, 2011.

Harder, Bernie. "Weaving Cultural Values on the Loom of Language." Media Development. London, World Association for Christian Communication. March,1989.

Hofstede, Geert. Cultures and Organizations: New York:McGraw-Hill. 1991.

Hostede, Geert. Culture's Consequences: Interntional Differences in Work-Related Values. London, New Delhi: Sage Publications, 1980.

Keller, Timothy. The Reason for God. New York: Riverhead Books, 2009.

Koessler, John. "Worship of the Trajectory," Carol Stream, Illinois: Christianity Today, vol. 55, no. 3, March 2011.

McLuhan, Marshall. The Gutenberg Galaxy. Toronto: Univrsity of Toronto Press, 1966.

McLuhan, Marshall. The Medium is the Massage. New York: Random House, 1967.

Olson, Bruce. Bruchko. Lake Mary, Florida: Charisma House, 2006.

Sahlins, Marshall. How "Natives" Think. Chicago and London: The University of Chicago Press, 1995.

Smith, Donald K. Creating Understanding: Christian Communiction Across Cultural Landscapes. Grand Rapids, MI., Zondervan. 1992.

Webber, Robert. Rappings. Wheaton, Illinois: Tyndale House,1971.

§

Endorsements

"Many missionaries and cross-cultural workers today get very little advance exposure to the realities and vagaries of culture before being asked to navigate within a new one. In a 'flat,' global world, some who deploy cross-cultural workers don't feel such equipping is as necessary as it was before. But sadly, many of those Ill-equipped workers quickly drop below the 'go-home' line. Many never recover, spending their entire (often short) overseas careers confused and frustrated. Don Smith has always been one who believed that workers will be more effective when they understand culture – what makes people tick; what makes them different – and special. For better communication, effectiveness and satisfaction, cross-cultural workers today need to discover again the wonders and beauties of culture. This book provides some of the best and most readable, entertaining, and valuable insights into culture I've seen anywhere. Read it. Enjoy it. Live it."

Dr. Dan Brewster,
Director, Academic Programs,
Compassion International. _Malaysia_

"Make haste slowly!

If you did not experience some of the frustrations, surprises or encounters you meet in '_Make Haste Slowly_' you have not been a missionary or development worker for any length of time.

Study it before you go abroad, return to it frequently during your service – and when years later you take it down from the bookshelf be reminded of forgotten events where the book made a positive difference in your work."

Flemming Kramp,
Former General Secretary,
Danish Missionary Council

"In every generation, our Sovereign Lord appears to select His choice servants who bring into focus and freshness old truths and practices He has purposed for that generation. Dr.Donald Smith is one of such fore-runners, qualified through his journey in the disciplines of Education and Communication, and enhanced through over 30 years of cross – cultural missionary work in Africa.

In the book *"Make Haste Slowly"*, Dr.Smith recaptures old methodologies used in passing down knowledge and information among the peoples of the Two Third world. Using his skills in communication and understanding of educational approaches in Africa, he introduced a model of training using the inductive story telling method, which is native to and natural within the environments most of missionary Trainees are being prepared to serve.

This book is a must reading for every Missions professional and practitioner, from both ends of the missionary spectrum (old and new sending)."

Dr. Seth Kofi Anyomi,
Ghana

"I am honored to have had Dr. Donald K. Smith as my professor at Western Seminary and as my Pastor at Faith Baptist Church during the early nineties in Portland, Oregon. He has been my model, mentor and prayer partner. His life has inspired and influenced me even as I serve the Lord in the North East India. *Make Haste Slowly* is an outcome of three decades of grass-root practical experience in communicating the Good News of salvation in Africa. This book is a must read as a handbook for all who are intending to serve the Lord in the cross-cultural context. With this ninth edition, the book is much more comprehensive both in theory and practical ways of communication. I recommend this book to mission practitioners and organizations that are involve in cross-cultural missions."

Dr. J.M. Ngul Khan Pau,
Senior Consultant,
Development Associates International, India

"In 1983 the Sudan Programme of Norwegian Church Aid, based in Torit, East Equatoria was at a crucial juncture. The Sudan People's Liberation Army (SPLA) was actively threatening all development agencies to stop working and leave the country. Very fortunately our Sudanese and expatriate staff had trained and worked with Donald K. Smith in how to *"Make Haste Slowly"*. As Director, I was able to lead our team to make decisive changes in direction and priorities and introduce a Sudanese management team and style that carried on successfully till the final evacuation in 1986. What was never lost in the following war was the change in thinking and approach introduced by Don Smith: Changing cultures from within!

Today (2011) the young nation of South Sudan is blessed with Ministers, Directors, Bishops, Pastors and business leaders who all recall the 1983 to 1986 training and practice as vital for their present participation in building the new nation. When you read this book you will understand why it made such an impact then, and why it continues to inspire new generations of development practitioners."

Oddvar Espegren,
Director, Christian Relief Network,
Norway and East Africa

"I am pleased that *Make Haste Slowly* has been published in a revised and expanded format. Long a valuable tool for cross cultural workers in East and Central Africa, the new edition offers a broader readership the insights and time-tested principles for communicating cross culturally that Don Smith has refined over decades of teaching, research and interaction with people from around the globe. I highly recommend this book to anyone who desires to communicate more effectively, whether in their own culture or another."

Dr. Garry Morgan,
Professor of Intercultural Studies and
Director of Global Initiatives, Northwestern College,
St. Paul, Minnesota, <u>USA</u>

"The summer of 1983 took me on a five week journey to the interior of East Africa: the Rukwa Region of western Tanzania, the town of Sumbawanga. I was a guest of the Norwegian government. I thought I had descended into the American wild west of the 1870s. There was violence, diseases long since abolished in the developed nations, and a very different work ethic.

My host, an employee of the government agency Norwegian Church Aid, briefed me that the reason they were there was because hydrologists and geologists from another Norwegian agency, while excellent engineers, were failing to establish and sustain sources of clean water for remote Tanzanian rural communities. It was a failure of communication, compounded by the technical correctness of well trained engineers. This conflict quickly affected relations between members of the two Norwegian government agencies. My host invited Don Smith to help sort out not only the challenges to cross-cultural communications between Tanzanians and Norwegians, but also the challenges between professional engineers and public health professionals.

The three day workshop greatly influenced me in the decades to come. In that time I have been employed by two national governments and directly dealt with representatives of three other national governments. This included permanent overseas residence and extended temporary duty, some during major international predicaments. The principles identified in *Make Haste Slowly* effectively aided my own efforts to adapt, cope, and deal with the challenges of communication with others from other cultures; sometimes when those cultures were solely defined as people of different professions.

Make Haste Slowly is written for an educated lay audience, and is well suited to the professional, government employee, or relief agency worker who will soon find themselves in a part of the world never before experienced."

Dan S. Sharp, MD, Ph.D.
(Public Health Physician and Epidemiologist)
USA

§

Donald K. Smith has taught, researched and guided cultural research in nearly 100 nations, primarily in Africa and Asia, focusing on communication. In 30 years of African residence, the Smiths co-founded Daystar University in Nairobi, Kenya, trained and supervised Bible translation teams, published a major Christian magazine (South Africa) and literacy materials in Ndebele and Shona (Zimbabwe), and counseled major development work in South Sudan. He chaired the Division of Intercultural Studies of Western Seminary, Portland, Oregon, USA. The Smiths began WorldView Center under the umbrella of the Institute for International Christian Communication, based in Portland, Oregon, USA. They have recently returned to permanent ministry at Daystar University in Kenya. His books include **Creating Understanding** and **Make Haste Slowly**. Smith holds B.S., M.S., M.A., Ph.D., and Litt.D. degrees.